# ILLOGICAL

## ALSO BY EMMANUEL ACHO

*Uncomfortable Conversations with a Black Man*

*Uncomfortable Conversations with a Black Boy*

# ILLOGICAL

SAYING YES TO A LIFE
WITHOUT LIMITS

# EMMANUEL ACHO

FLATIRON
BOOKS
NEW YORK

AN
OPRAH
BOOK

www.flatironbooks.com

Designed by Donna Sinisgalli Noetzel

The Library of Congress Cataloging-in-Publication Data is
available upon request.

ISBN 978-1-250-83644-1 (hardcover)
ISBN 978-1-250-83645-8 (ebook)

Our books may be purchased in bulk for promotional,
educational, or business use. Please contact your local
bookseller or the Macmillan Corporate and Premium Sales
Department at 1-800-221-7945, extension 5442, or by email at
MacmillanSpecialMarkets@macmillan.com.

First Edition: 2022

10   9   8   7   6   5   4   3   2   1

To those eager to do the extra and
become extraordinary

# Contents

# ILLOGICAL

# Imagine a life

## without limits. . . .

# Introduction

# Pins or Screws?

n March 2015, I was feeling great about my future in the National Football League. We were between seasons waiting for drafts, cuts, and re-signs to make up next year's team, but I wasn't worried about my place on the field. I was the guy, rated the thirty-third overall linebacker in a league of thirty-two teams, each with two starting linebackers—I deserved another year with the Philadelphia Eagles. I knew I could hang and I felt sure my team knew it, too.

Being sure was all the sweeter because I had been cut the year before. Then, I'd had a feeling it was coming. The coach had his favorites and I was not one of them, no matter how well I performed. I invited my parents to the final game of the preseason because I suspected it might be my last chance to show them that, yes, I could play pro ball. I led the team in tackles that day. But sure enough, the next morning, after I left brunch with my parents, my phone rang. It was Howie Roseman, the general manager. He told me to return my playbook; the team was releasing me. "It's not that you're not fast," he began, "we just found someone a little bit faster. It's not that you're not strong," he continued, "we just found someone a little bit stronger. It's not that you're not quick," he concluded, "we just found someone a little bit quicker." I laughed to keep from crying.

Two weeks later, after one of the starters suffered an injury, they re-signed me. And even though there were three other linebackers ahead of me on the roster, I started that game and finished the 2014 season as a starter. I was more prepared, a better player.

By March 2015, I felt sure even the politics of favoritism couldn't hold me back.

Then everything changed.

I had complained about continued pain in my thumb earlier in the week, after a sprain during a pre-season game. (A thumb sprain may not sound debilitating to you, but when your job is to grapple with three-hundred-pound men, trust me, it can be.) An X-ray showed there was no fracture, but I knew something was wrong. Due to the demands of the NFL, however, I suited up for the next game, and three plays in, I heard a pop.

The pain was unbearable. Both physically and emotionally. I realized I had likely broken my thumb, but worse than that, I had shattered my dream. If the break was major, the doctors would need to put pins into my thumb to keep the bone together. I had been injured before, so I knew that the amount of hardware in my hand would determine the extent of my rehab. Pins would protrude out of the skin and cause me to miss more than four weeks, over a quarter of the season. If the break was minor, though, screws would be placed on the bone under the skin and I could be back playing in a week or two, just in time for the start of the regular season.

After I came out of surgery, I asked my doctor one question: "Pins or screws?"

His answer would determine whether the team would see me as expendable and use my roster spot on someone else—ending not only my season and time with the Eagles, but most likely my entire NFL career—or whether they would keep me on the roster for the season. Sure I might have to play with a club on my hand, but the check would cash and my job status would be secure.

"Pins or screws?" I asked again. His answer: "Pins."

I knew what was coming. A few moments later, my phone rang. It was the GM, the same person who had called me the year before, telling me again that it was time to go. I got up off the operating table, took off my gown, and caught a ride back to the team's practice facility.

I was less than an hour removed from surgery and still foggy from the pain meds, but upon arrival I was asked to return my playbook and empty my locker immediately. I turned in my team-issued iPad and received, in exchange, a large black garbage bag. I awkwardly opened my locker with my left hand—my right hand heavily bandaged and punctured with pins—and item by item dumped out the memorabilia into this black hole. As the bag filled up, my emptiness increased.

I spent the next few weeks rehabbing and the subsequent months training, waiting for a call from an NFL team, any team. I remember stealing some traffic cones from a parking lot in Philly and using them to do drills in the alley behind my apartment. I found empty fields to train on. My former teammates were making millions; I was making ends meet with the severance check the team gave me when they sent me packing. It was embarrassing. Though I was not seeing a psychologist at the time, the word "depressed" crossed my mind on more than one occasion. It was dark, cold, and lonely, and I had no end in sight. My friends in the NFL were busy playing and my non-football friends didn't live in Philly. I was alone. I was sad. I didn't know where to go.

It all felt like something I'd feared my whole life: failure. From the injury, to the release, to the solo workouts—I saw the life I'd worked so hard to attain, the success I'd competed for with my whole body, mind, and soul, slipping away. And though it wouldn't be the last time I stepped on an NFL field as a football player, it was a major turning point in my life.

During that time, I had a decision to make. I could either do the logical thing: sit, train, and wait for a team to call me back—or I could do the illogical thing: pour all that energy into something completely new that I had no experience in. Eventually, I made up my mind to choose the latter and decided to pursue a career in media. Prior to this I had put my head down, worked hard, sacrificed my individuality for the sake of the team, but now I knew I needed to step out, use my voice, and share what was inside of me with the larger world. This decision changed everything. Instead of chasing a dashed dream, I began to believe in my heart there was something more to me. More to my story. I just needed to be brave enough not to follow old patterns and instead reach for new ones. I needed to be illogical.

A little over two years later, I rejoined the Eagles to celebrate the Super Bowl. Except this time, it wasn't as an NFL player, it was as a television analyst.

Fast-forward to July 2020. After the tragic murder of George Floyd, I got another call from the Eagles' general manager, now asking for my advice. The team wanted to make a statement but didn't know what to say, so they asked me for help because I had been using my voice and platform to speak out against racism and I was now well-versed in the media landscape. They let me take control of their statement and make edits as I saw fit. I did. That same GM, the one who allowed me to be cut five times before I turned twenty-five, would call me again a few weeks later asking me to come speak to the entire team about how best to stand for justice in the midst of our world's turmoil. My illogical path led me straight to my truest calling.

Before we go any further, let's start with a working definition of what logic actually is. "Logic," for the purpose of this book, is conventional wisdom. The thoughts, beliefs, and opinions held by the majority of people around you. But let's break it down even further. The word "conventional" is derived from the word "convention." What is convention? Our friends at Merriam-Webster tell us it's "a general agreement about basic principles or procedures." "Wisdom" is simply defined as "the fact of being based on sensible thinking." Putting the pieces together, conventional wisdom is "a general agreement about basic principles or procedures based on sensible thinking."

Let's get historical for a second. For hundreds of years now, women have unfortunately been forced to chase ever-evasive standards of beauty. As soon as society has settled on one definition, it changes. This change subliminally forces women to adapt to the change and men to alter their taste in order to follow the mold of society. Allow me to prove it to you. The Italian Renaissance from 1400 to 1700 is known for connecting the ancient world to the modern world. It was the age in which the printing press, eyeglasses, and even the flush toilet were created. But the Renaissance era was also known for a distinct taste in beauty, vastly different from what we appreciate now. For a woman to be deemed "beautiful" in the Renaissance era she had to be pale with full hips, a full chest, and a rounded body. Interestingly enough, a high forehead was also a necessary ingredient to meet the epitome of beauty standards.

Two weeks ago, I took a trip to Paris, and while there I of course had to journey to the Eiffel Tower and the famous Louvre Museum. The Louvre blew me away with the artwork not only on the walls, but even the designs on the ceiling. Thousands of people walked the halls and stairs of the museum taking in all of the distinct creations, but only one painting commanded a line of people—a line so long that I decided not to wait in it, but rather walk around and see what all the fuss was about. I wondered what was so captivating that hundreds would choose to wait in line for one painting amidst a museum full of brilliant creations. As I walked toward the front I finally saw what everyone had been waiting on. It was the *Mona Lisa* (painted between 1503 and 1519). The *Mona Lisa* is one of the most famous paintings known to man. The half-length portrait of Lisa Gherardini has been featured in hip-hop songs, and there have been movies made sharing its title. But if the *Mona Lisa* were painted today, it would likely end up for purchase at your local garage sale. Not because it is not an incredible work of art, but because Lisa Gherardini was a pale woman with a seemingly large forehead and thin lips. Pale complexion, thin lips, and a large forehead are now seen as strikes against you when it comes to 2021's beauty standards. In 2021, the beauty of a woman is defined by sun-kissed skin, and you are expected to be skinny, but not too skinny. Stomach must be flat, but breasts should be large along with the butt; however, the waist should be small. An impossible physical paradox for most. From the 1400s to the 2000s, the world's standards of "beauty" have changed many times. Tall, short, round, thin, busty, and flat have all come and gone. And some have come again.

From birth, society tells us what beauty is, what success is, even what happiness looks like. But why do we let insignificant people have such significance in our lives? Think about it. Somewhere along the way, during the early 1400s, a few people (likely men) decided what "beauty" looked like. And everyone else subscribed to their definition. Then, a few hundred years later, another group of people got together and defined beauty. We then mindlessly chased that definition, and this cycle has repeated itself and will continue to repeat itself until the end of time. Society teaches us to toil toward a goal we can never reach, like hamsters in a wheel, and by the time we get close the goal has changed. So what is the solution?

Get off of the wheel.

If we chase a standard of beauty that someone else has set for us, imagine what else in life we long for even though its value has been defined by someone other than you. As I'm writing this book, the 2021 Olympic Games in Tokyo have recently concluded. Many athletes stood with jubilation atop the podiums that boast the top three finishers. Their necks were adorned with medals: gold, silver, and bronze, respectively. A fourth-place finish is arguably the worst pain an athlete can endure on the Olympic stage, but why? Because somewhere along the way value was assigned only to the top three finishers of their sport. If you finished fourth, well, you failed. In reality, what is the difference between third and fourth? A few points maybe, a tenth of a second, a penalty kick. Either way, it's nothing so drastic that it should undermine the success of athletes that are already greater than everyone else in the world. However, every four years (occasionally five during a global pandemic) we see this happen.

Let me break it down even further for you. The National Basketball Association ends each basketball season with the NBA Finals, a best-of-seven contest between two teams where the first team to win four games gets the trophy. The second-place team leaves the court with heads held low and tears in their eyes. They have lost it all. They have failed. However, the exact same sport and the exact same second-place finish will yield a much different emotional response at the Olympic Games. Because at some point in time (1904 to be exact), second-place finishers were told they had value at the Olympics. But still, in the NBA, second-place finishers are as irrelevant as the last-place finisher. It's truly mind-blowing to think about. The exact same finish in the exact same sport will yield a totally different emotional response because of what some people from 1904 decided!

Let's personalize it. LeBron James is in a two-person race to become the greatest basketball player of all time. The race is between him and Michael Jordan. Michael Jordan has won six NBA championships while Lebron has won only four; however, LeBron has six second-place finishes, while Jordan never amassed any second-place finishes. Michael Jordan either won the championship, or did not come close. But never second. The greatest argument against LeBron James is the fact that he's lost more NBA championships than he's won. Similarly, the greatest argument in favor of Michael Jordan is that he never lost an NBA championship he played in. Based upon the "goals" that the NBA has set, Michael Jordan clearly has the advantage as a winner. But if you take the exact same athletes and the exact same results and apply them to the Olympic metric of success, LeBron would clearly be supreme. LeBron has amassed four first-place finishes and six second-place finishes, while Jordan has six first-place finishes. All of this is to say, who is "greatest" between the two athletes is all dependent upon which archaic metric created by someone else years ago you wish to subscribe to. I say we should unsubscribe.

Stop letting your value, your success, or even your greatness be determined by someone other than you. Especially someone you don't know. Stop letting your beauty, your happiness, or your worth be dependent upon the convention of the time. You are valuable, worthy, and beautiful. We all are. We just have to assess ourselves based on the metric that matters most—our own. Once you've realized that your standards are the only ones by which you should measure anything, then you can take full agency over your life. You can take the power back from the society which took it from you at birth.

We were raised with certain ideologies and limitations engrained into our minds by society and we just accepted them to be true. A black man could never be president, we were told. A woman could never be the CEO of a Fortune 500 company. And a black woman, ha! There's no way she could become a billionaire. We all fall victim to these limitations except for the select few who realize that the wisdom of someone else may be foolishness to them.

In the 1999 science-fiction film *The Matrix*, the main character, Neo, has a unique encounter with a character known as "Spoon Boy." Neo sits in the waiting room of the Oracle waiting to be told if he is indeed the chosen one who is believed will save humanity. While he waits, he sees a boy sitting legs crossed with several bent spoons in front of him. He doesn't think much of it until he witnesses the boy hold a spoon in front of his face and bend the spoon only by looking at it. Neo stares in amazement and the small boy then offers Neo the spoon as if to say, "Here, you can do it, too." Neo receives the spoon from the boy, confused. He's not sure where to begin. (I get it, I've never bent a spoon with my mind either.) As Neo holds the spoon, staring at it with confusion, the boy says, "Do not try and bend the spoon. That's impossible. Instead only try to realize the truth." Neo responds, "What truth?" To which the boy answers, "There is no spoon. . . . It is not the spoon that bends, it is only yourself." Neo then holds the spoon in front of his own face and stares intently, as the spoon begins to bend and he is summoned into the Oracle's office.

While this movie is fiction, the application of this scene is very real. A spoon can't bend without an external physical force; that is scientifically impossible. It is also impossible for you or I to ever measure up to the standard of beauty the world has set for us. It is impossible to be successful enough or great enough according to someone or something else. But we must apply the same truth to our lives that Spoon Boy told Neo in the scene of my favorite movie growing up. It is not the things around you that bend, only yourself.

We may not be able to bend the standards of society. We may not be able to bend the metrics of greatness that others set hundreds of years before we were even born. We may not even be able to bend how others see us. But what we can do is bend how we see ourselves. We can bend our perception of what it means to be valuable, to be successful, or to be beautiful.

We adopt far too many values and beliefs from someone else. It's not just the large ideologies either. We even do this with the small things—a banana, for example. We've been engrained since birth to believe that the long stem was the top and thus that's how we peel them, starting from the top. However, what we consider the bottom of the banana is actually the top, as bananas grow from the stem upward. So yes, you've been eating bananas wrong your whole life based upon indoctrination.

Let's think about the spoon again for a second, and no, we're not bending it this time. A spoon is actually a much better utensil to use when eating a rice dish, so why do we use a fork? A fork allows the grains of rice to escape whereas a spoon does not. But society tells us to use a fork to eat all dishes that are primarily dry in substance. So that is what we do.

I've challenged everything from how you think to how you eat to remind you that at best, you could be living life inefficiently. At worst, you could be doing life all wrong. No, everything in life is not truly meaningless, but the only meaning anything in your life should have is the meaning you give it. From here on, take agency over your view of life. Take control over what is valuable in your life. Take the power back from society. Step off the hamster wheel and bend the spoon. Just remember, it's not the spoon that bends, only yourself.

To bend ourselves, we must be illogical.

———————
———————
———————

Funnily enough, I tend to be highly logical. That trait has taken me far. It has helped me approach situations looking for rational, reasonable resolutions. But it has also threatened to limit me if I leaned into it too much. I had to make the leap to illogical by realizing that there is more to life than conventional wisdom can offer. I changed my way of thinking and started asking myself, "But what if it is possible?" "What if I can bend the spoon?" I exchanged thoughts of "I can't" with thoughts of "I will." Logic in and of itself isn't bad, but faith is better than fear. Especially when logic is the limiting factor.

I'm here for one simple reason: to tell you that the basic principles or procedures you've been living by haven't been working. Why? Because they were never meant to. If you dig a bit deeper, you'll find a few other definitions for "conventional." You'll see statements like "lacking originality or individuality," "commonplace," even "ordinary." You were not meant to be ordinary. And you sure as heck weren't meant to be logical. Let's fight against this trap of being ordinary. Let's fight against the mundane life that we may find ourselves mindlessly living, together.

Like I said, life can change quickly. Losses pile up and wins can seem few and far between. But what I learned from my time with the Eagles, and so many other times when life took an unexpected turn, is that we've got to start playing a different game; to start playing by different rules, our own rules. Even when society deems them illogical and attempts to walk you down the logical path. You may not be the favorite; you may get fired, get injured, get let go. But your story isn't over. If you can let yourself envision something different, your story may just be beginning.

I've learned a lot of lessons in my illogical life, and I share them in this book. It's not easy to shrug off the mantle of the world's wisdom. It takes courage and perseverance every step of the way. Each chapter is a truth I've found essential to keep in mind and I hope these truths will help you, too. This isn't about me, but about all of us. In these pages you'll see stories from some of my many illogical heroes: people who, in ways large and small, personal and global, didn't let conventional wisdom stand in their way.

We must know how and when to change the rules of the game. It's time to not let the goals we set for ourselves, or that others set for us, limit what we can imagine. We must not let others' fears become our own because their words "make sense" in societally conventional ways. We must rethink what we call success or failure—even thinking beyond "failure" entirely. This book will teach you how to, as I call it, be illogical. To live your unique truth. And by doing so, live a life without limits.

The only meaning
anything in your life
should have is the
meaning you give it.

 #illogicalbook

# 1

## Before the Cards Are Flipped

It was the middle of the summer and "The Kid" was sitting in the back room of the Sugar House with more than $20,000 on the table. "The cards are the cards," he said, cracking a smile. I was nervous. I couldn't stop tapping my measly twenty-five-dollar chip on the wooden frame of the table. The Kid seemed unfazed. He doubled down on his bet, leaned back in his chair, and allowed himself to relax. He had it all under control.

While in the NFL, I frequented casinos more often than I'd care to admit; everybody has their thing. For me, the friends I made at the different gambling tables filled the void left by having no family near me during my playing career. That along with the excitement of winning a game of chance. The joy of victory and the agony of defeat could seemingly both be experienced in a matter of minutes. Complete strangers sharing hugs and embraces (pre-COVID, of course) after a big win, or collective sighs of frustration after the loss of a hand. High risk, high reward. It was invigorating. I made many memories during those visits, but the most unforgettable of them all came the day I took a trip to play blackjack with The Kid.

The game of blackjack is simple. For those of you who have never seen the movie *21*, I'll explain. You are dealt two cards and left with one decision. Ask for more or stick with what you've got. The object of the game is for your total card value to be at or as close to twenty-one as possible. You're competing against the dealer, so whoever is closer to twenty-one wins. Aces are worth one or eleven, face cards ten, and number cards are worth the number shown on the cards, two through ten. You take the cards you're dealt. You can't change them. But you can ask for more. You can take a risk to try and get closer to a win. The only issue with this risk is that it comes with a clause, the chance that you could bust. Busting is when the value of your cards rises above twenty-one. When that happens, you lose, the dealer wins, and you're out of the game. High risk, high reward.

In the back room at the Sugar House, The Kid decided to double down, meaning that his $20,000 bet would yield him an additional $20,000. He had $40,000 at stake; enough money to make a down payment on a small Philadelphia townhouse. It also meant that he was choosing to take a major risk to accept one card, and one card only, from the dealer. I was familiar with the idea of doubling down, but not with the cards that The Kid was showing. His hand showed two fours, a total value of eight. The dealer had two cards as well. His top card was an eight and his bottom card was facedown. Advantage, dealer. Or so I thought. No matter what, The Kid wasn't getting to twenty-one. I already told y'all the value of every card, and there is no card valued at thirteen in the game. But for whatever reason, he still made the decision. He liked his odds.

While in the NFL, I took a sports analytics class as part of my graduate degree. My professor was from Philly, a Temple University alum who was familiar with the Sugar House. For my final project, I chose to focus on odds and the game of blackjack. After all, you pursue an education to learn, but also to increase your chances of making money, right? I spent roughly one hundred hours studying the odds of nearly every potential hand in blackjack. Talk about real-life application.

Based on my formal education, The Kid's odds were slim. I knew that, the dealer knew that, everyone at the table knew that. But The Kid chose not to believe it. He leaned back, cracked a smirk, and looked at me as he said, "The cards are the cards," assuring the dealer that he was confident in his decision. The dealer pulled a final card out of the deck and slid it to The Kid. "Facedown!" my teammate urged, hoping to build up the suspense of the moment. The dealer slid the unknown card beneath the two fours. The cards were indeed the cards, and nothing at this point could change the result: $40,000 was on the line. I was as nervous as if it were my money, but The Kid seemed unfazed.

Imagine the confidence you'd need to keep cool during something like this. If The Kid was sweating, no one noticed. Everything in his demeanor oozed swagger. No stress, no anxiety, no doubt. He trusted his gut and wasn't afraid. As I studied his cool demeanor, I realized that the most stressful times in our lives often occur before the cards are even flipped. We've calculated our odds and it feels like we have no chance. We worry, we fret, we panic. We don't know what's coming next, so we break. We abort. We run away before the game plays out. But that night at the casino, I learned that life doesn't have to be so logical. Even in the face of stacked odds, you can own the moment. You can be confident even when you don't know what comes next, or when you fear the worst comes next because of what logic tells you. You can take risks and trust that it's going to be okay.

I recently spoke with a friend who was going through a major transition. In many ways, he was waiting for his cards to be flipped. He was scared, confused, even a bit intimidated by the unknown that awaited him as he approached a new life stage. He was changing jobs and didn't know what the future held. I reminded him about a truth that I had learned that day at the casino: when uncertainty hits, go with it. You have an opportunity, in whatever you do, to create. To be different. To not be concerned about the calculations or the odds. To be illogical enough to believe that you can do something that's never been done.

The dealer flipped the other house card over. It was a ten of hearts. The Kid's hope was all but lost. The dealer now had a value of eighteen to The Kid's eight. And while The Kid still had his own card to turn over, only one would give him victory. Four cards would yield a draw and the final seven cards would net a loss of the average annual salary in America. To put it plainly, there was roughly a 7 percent chance that The Kid would win, a 31 percent chance The Kid would tie, and a 62 percent chance that The Kid's pockets would be a lot lighter. I gently placed my hand on The Kid's shoulder, preparing to comfort him for what would surely be a significant loss.

The Kid looked up at the dealer and signaled him permission to flip the final card. The room was silent, each person on the edge of their seat. The dealer flipped The Kid's card over, slowly but with intent. It was the moment of truth. The last play of the game. A final opportunity. I braced myself. The card hit the table, followed shortly by my jaw. The crowd erupted. The Kid had done it. He'd drawn the one card he'd needed to win, an ace, giving him a total value of nineteen. Strangers reached across the table high-fiving each other. I was screaming in excitement and people were hugging me as if I had been the one to win. The Kid, however, ignored all the gestures around him. He just looked at me, nodded his head ever so slightly, and gave me a wink.

We collected our chips and headed to the cashier. The Kid could hardly hold on to each of the five-thousand-dollar pieces of plastic. As I waited in line for him to cash out, I gently mumbled a question that I couldn't shake: "You know you only had a seven percent chance to win the hand, right?"

He paused briefly, still dismayed at my lack of belief. He then sighed and responded, "Acho . . . sometimes you're too smart for your own good."

While life is no game of blackjack, we all have a choice to make. Will we take a chance on our dreams regardless of their supposed success rate? Will we show up to the table? Will we go for it all and live the life we deserve, or will we let logic deter us from our greatness?

In my darkest days after being let go from the Philadelphia Eagles, I almost let logic swallow me. I loved football. I'd worked hard at it. Everyone around me told me that playing in the NFL was the opportunity of a lifetime—was *my* opportunity of a lifetime. It was hard to stop pursuing the dream that I felt I was best suited for, but that door was slammed in my face. I was forced to find another way forward, the alternative being to continue expending my energy ramming into the door simply because it was what I was supposed to do.

So I turned away from the door. I believed in my heart of hearts that there was something more for me. More to my story, like there is more to yours. I just needed to be brave enough to create it. To believe that when the card was flipped, I would still be okay.

I always knew I wanted to communicate. I love helping people see the best in themselves and bringing out the best in me as well. I wanted to refine my skills as a speaker, so after each day of training, I went home, took a shower, and began the task of calling everyone I knew to see what opportunities were out there. A few months later, I found myself on the set of the Longhorn Network, a college football TV station that covered any and all things related to the University of Texas, my alma mater.

Illogical decision number one was leaving the NFL before the final nail was in the coffin. Imagine that—retiring from the game of football, my first job, when I was twenty-five. I was still young enough that I could have waited longer, prepared more, hoped for that dream to stay alive. Instead, I was going into the unknown.

Illogical decision number two was believing I could succeed on the Longhorn Network. My seat was fixed between two heroes of the state of Texas, with Heisman Trophies to their names along with entire fields and restaurants that bore their appellation. They had both played in the NFL much longer than me, and had achieved more collegiate accolades than I could have ever imagined. Still, I saw an opportunity. I knew that I would have to work harder than ever before, but I was ready for a new challenge.

Week in and week out, I trained, but this time for something different. I watched recordings of the best analysts on TV and took notes on their different styles. I studied the work of other effective communicators and orators, implementing things that I liked from their skill sets into mine. Whether it was a rapper, a musician, a business leader, or a media mogul, I found valuable lessons in all of them. I was willing to learn from anyone. I even learned from Taylor Swift. I love music, but I'm not much of a concertgoer. Big crowds just aren't my thing. But I've been to one life-changing concert in my life. I'm not obsessed with Taylor Swift's music and truly we couldn't be more different—I am a black man who played pro sports and she is a white woman specializing in country and pop music—but I am enthralled by her genius. When I was offered free tickets to see her show at the Philadelphia Eagles stadium in her home state of Pennsylvania, I jumped at the opportunity. It was a little uncomfortable—I knew I didn't necessarily fit the mold of her average fan, but I was eager to see her perform. Upon arrival, everyone was given a wristband. I had no idea what the wristbands were for as they were clear, made of plastic, and seemingly useless. However, one hour into the concert, my mind was blown. As Taylor began to perform her Grammy-winning song "Bad Blood," the entire stadium lit up red and white. It was then that I realized the value of the wristbands: they allowed us to be her co-performers. She has found a way to captivate the hearts of millions around the world and to make her fans feel like more than just spectators. I learned that day that it's not enough to entertain a crowd, but that you have to engage them as well. You too can discover new ideas from those who look different, sound different, and work completely different jobs than you. Don't be afraid to step out of your comfort zone.

Those two years at Longhorn Network were a grind. I traveled nonstop while many of my peers continued to play professionally. They were on practice fields, I was on planes. They were on primetime TV, I was on public transportation. I worked in four different cities, at three different stations, six days a week. If I wasn't working, I was traveling to work. If I wasn't traveling to work, I was thinking about work. I was dreaming, planning, plotting ways I could earn my keep—ways I could keep on creating. Success, my friends, doesn't come overnight, however you define it.

After two years of a schedule so brutal I woke up in hotel rooms confused as to what city I was in, I was asked to join ESPN, the network referred to as "the worldwide leader in sports." I was set to be the youngest national football analyst to grace the platform. I obliged. By this point, I knew not to take a conventional measure of success like a job promotion to mean I'd made it—that I could stop thinking outside the box about what I wanted to do and what I wanted my life to be.

Everything I had learned during my four years in the NFL translated to my new career. The mental and physical toughness, the resilience, the determination—all of the traits I refined while playing professional football were paying off in a different way. My illogical decision to leave the NFL and dive into broadcasting, young and untested, was beginning to make perfect sense *for me*. Step by step I got more comfortable with the uncertainty. I befriended the unknown. I tried new things and allowed my creativity to flow freely. Did I make a mistake every now and then? Of course, and I promise you will too. But I was no longer afraid to fail. Why? Because I'd lived through failure and now I could sit with the uncertainty before the card was flipped. I realized while I waited to see if my gamble paid off or not that **failure is simply an opportunity to try something new**.

And my gamble did pay off, because I was able to sit in the uncertainty and walk down an illogical path not knowing what was at the end. Another couple of years later, I was hosting my own show, on a new network, every day of the week. Shortly thereafter, I found myself on the phone with Oprah Winfrey and in chairs across from Matthew McConaughey, Roger Goodell, and an entire city's police department. Then I was on the *New York Times* bestseller list and giving a speech after winning an Emmy award. But these are all stories for later. The upshot is that the millions of viewers I've been able to connect with, and the countless important—and uncomfortable—conversations I've been able to have, all began with my willingness to be illogical. To leave the game, and then to change it. This, my friends, is my vision for you.

You may not think you're ready to be illogical. I agree. We're never ready. Much like having a child, being a spouse, and even starting a new business or going back to school, you're never really ready. But when it's time, it's time. And now, my friends, it's time.

It starts with your mind. We each have a beautiful mind. An ability to believe. The freedom to think for ourselves. To form a new opinion about our future.

What's next? After what we all have comes what only *you* have. Your skills, your passions, your intrinsic gifts, your ideas. You may not be an athlete or a public speaker just as I'm not a graceful dancer or a math whiz. The point is that comparisons are irrelevant.

We're all worth believing in. Albert Einstein said it best: "Everybody is a genius. But if you judge a fish by its ability to climb a tree, it will live its whole life believing that it is stupid." So, let's start with two key beliefs as we embark on our illogical path: You are as ready as you will ever be, and in your own unique way, you are a genius. Maybe not in the traditional sense based on some aptitude test you have twelve minutes to take, but you are exceptionally skilled at something. Let's go on a journey and discover it together.

Once you've decided what you're willing to be illogical about—the deep-down stuff in you that's worth believing in, no matter what—there will be a lot of hard work. And probably a lot of failure. (But remember, we've redefined failure as opportunity.) What you need to know from the start is that you— right now, you as you're reading this—don't need to be any smarter, or more qualified, or any of those terms of convention. You are enough just as you are. You don't follow your calling because you're qualified. You qualify by following your calling. Believe that you can create something beautiful. Something magnificent. Something majestic for the world to see. Being illogical means having the courage to believe that you—yes, you—have everything you've ever needed to do what you were put on this earth to do.

Logic limits, and you were meant to fly.

Logically, the Wright brothers weren't supposed to invent an object that could fly through the air while carrying people in it. Logically, Steve Jobs was not supposed to create a device that could simultaneously act as a camera, music player, phone, and much more. Logically, Martin Luther King Jr. was not supposed to believe that he could stand in the gap and speak up against America's biggest sin.

It's time to become *illogical* and push the limits on what life has to offer. Look at that unflipped card as an invitation to something better. Let's defy logic, together.

Be Illogical:

**Take the chance.** Life is short and tomorrow is not promised. Do not live a half-filled life leaving yourself to wonder, "What if?" Just go do it.

**The greatest reward comes after the greatest risk.** There's a saying in the casino: "Scared money don't make no money." Meaning, if you want to win big, you have to bet big. The same principle exists in life. When you're illogical enough to believe you can do the impossible, the future will be uncertain, but the reward will be great.

**Logic limits.** Sometimes you've got to throw reason to the wind. It's not reasonable to think that man could ascend to the moon. It's not reasonable to think a device you can fit in your palm would allow you to communicate with people all over the world. But it wasn't reason that made those things possible. It was a dream followed by belief. Don't let logic limit your life.

Failure is simply

an opportunity to

**TRY SOMETHING NEW.**

# 2

## Childlike Faith

It takes a very long time to become young.

—PICASSO

I had just finished a workout and was sitting in my car, scrolling through social media. Part of me was trying to recover from the lift, part of me was checking to see what I had missed during my two-hour "get right" session. As I was seated, a car pulled up next to me. My trainer had come back from his lunch break and brought his daughter along. He didn't see me, but I saw him. He went to the back seat of the car, opened the door, and helped his five-year-old hop out of the vehicle. The kid was excited. A chance to go to work with her dad, a chance to see something new. In her excitement, she began to dash toward the workout facility. Before she could put her third step on the ground, her dad yelled, "Wait, there may be a car coming!" The girl immediately halted. There was no car. My trainer was just performing his parental duties and warning his daughter out of an abundance of caution.

It was an interesting interaction. The child didn't consider any potential danger around her. She didn't consider obstacles or threats that could get in her way. She just sprinted toward her desired destination. That moment nearly brought me to tears. It reminded me of the freedom that many children live with. Freedom from fear, trepidation, regret, or constantly wondering "What if?"

As children, we have a superpower: the ability to dream the impossible and move without fear of the consequences. But as we grow older and experience hardship, fear, and the expectations and prejudices of the world, this superpower dissipates. By the time we reach adolescence, this birthright is often completely gone. We become logical.

I'm confident that if you're reading this book, then you are over the age of five, but we all have a lesson to learn. A lesson about belief, a lesson about the childlike faith that little girl had as she rushed toward what she wanted.

I was recently at Altitude Trampoline Park with my friends and their young children. I waltzed into this theme park and immediately felt out of place because I was about twenty years older and two hundred pounds heavier than the average eight-year-old sprinting around the area in jubilation. At first, I sat there and took in the sights. Some kids were playing ping-pong on the tables near the entrance and others were playing air hockey, sending pucks everywhere, but the majority were on the trampolines. Kids were flying through the air, one backflip after another. A young girl even did a double backflip in the air—I swear she's the next Simone Biles.

As I sat there with my jaw hung low, a boy named

Chase invited me over to his trampoline. He greeted me with a smile and said, "Hey, mister, you want to try?"

I responded, "Oh no, you have your fun!"

But Chase was not taking no for an answer. He replied, "Come on, man, don't be scared."

Now picture me, roughly six foot two, 240 pounds, being egged on by this child who was barely four feet tall. I said to Chase, "Of course I'm not scared! Let me put my shoes away and I'll be right back!" I stashed my shoes at the cubbies and as I walked back toward Chase, I whispered under my breath, "He must not know who he just challenged. I'm a former NFL linebacker. Scared?! Me? Heck no. He doesn't know who he's talking to." Back at the trampoline, I was surprised to find a crowd of ten or so children awaiting me. I guessed Chase had summoned his friends to witness what was to come.

I parted the sea of children and took my place in the middle of the trampoline as the crowd hovered around me.

"Do a backflip!" they yelled. "We want to see you do a backflip."

I snickered. "Oh, that's it! Okay, I'll show y'all young-sters how it's done." There was only one problem—I hadn't done a backflip in roughly twenty years, since I was around Chase's age. I began to spring up and down in the air, gaining height as I tried to build up confidence. I told the children to count to three and on three I would do it.

"One, two—"

"Wait, wait, wait! Y'all are counting too fast!" I yelled before they got to three.

The children collectively shook their heads in annoyance and proceeded again. "One . . . two . . ."

"WAIT! WAIT!" I stopped them again. "My socks are too slick; I don't have enough traction."

A girl jeered from the crowd, "Stop being scared, I'll show you how it's done!" She walked up to the trampoline, took her place in front of me, and before I could blink, had done a flip as quick as it was graceful. She turned around, looked up into my eyes, and said, "See, easy. Your turn."

As she stepped off the trampoline, I began springing up and down again, building my confidence. The children did not count this time; it was simply assumed I would go when I was ready. There was one problem—I was never going to be ready. *What if I freak out in the air and can't stick the landing? What if I embarrass myself in front of all these kids?*

*They'll laugh me all the way out the front door.* These thoughts clouded my mind as I stalled, bouncing up and down. These thoughts stopped me.

The freedom I possessed as a child had matured into fear. I had become too calculated, too reasonable, too . . . logical. There was no way that I could propel my 240-pound frame backward through the air *and* land back on my feet. Yeah, that wasn't happening. Or at least, I had convinced myself there was no way I was strong enough or coordinated enough, but those were lies. I had worked out five days a week for the previous fifteen years and played professional sports—strength and coordination weren't the problem. The real problem: I wasn't bold enough. I had all the ability in the world, I had all the skills to execute the task, but I was missing the main ingredient. I had no faith, I had no belief. I was the exact thing that Chase and the other children warned me not to be: I was scared.

The longer you and I are on Earth, the more we focus on what we can't do as opposed to what we *can* do. When logic tells us that taking a risk means failure, the thing that's holding us back isn't our ability, it's our fear. Our fear that following the illogical path isn't safe, even if living a life that isn't true to ourselves is ultimately worse than taking a chance.

Remember, you have the creative genius, the mental ability, or the physical talent necessary. You just need the courage. You don't need anyone to count to three for you and you don't need a group of spectators (trust me, it's nerve-racking). Everything you need to achieve your dreams you already possess. **You just have to change your attitude in life because your attitude determines your altitude.**

Take a moment and think about your fears. The areas that give you pause. The jumps you've been too afraid to take. Think about the hesitancy that you feel when it's time for you to make the leap. Maybe it's a job change. Maybe it's a relationship that's evolving. Maybe it's a dream that has been tucked away deep in the recesses of your mind. You see, this is not just a me issue or a you issue. It's a we issue.

Maybe you've been hurt before. Maybe you've had your dreams shot down by people who know you well, or by those who don't know you at all. Remember this: Someone may know where you're from, but they have no idea where you're going, especially when you start to believe the impossible, when you start having childlike faith. Your faith is a muscle. It grows stronger every time you choose to believe the unbelievable. It expands when you refuse to let logic be your limiting factor. Your faith increases as you continue to make leaps in your life. Even if the leap opposes your logic, in fact especially if it does, it is worth it. Your dream is just around the corner, your freedom is just around the bend. Take the jump. Have faith.

Of course, childlike faith doesn't mean you don't have fears, it means you choose not to let your fears stop you from taking a leap. It means you talk openly about your fears with the ones who love you most. You share your fears with a close friend or a loved one, and if you're a person of religious faith, you share them with God. Conventional thinking tells us that when we move cities, change zip codes, switch schools, or shake something up, we lose something. It tells us that when we start afresh, things won't work out. But what we lose by not doing these things are the dreams that need to be fed and nourished if we are going to live full lives. Stop believing conventional thinking and start listening to your dreams, not your fears. Learn from the young people around us who take the world in with wonder and who are constantly looking to expand and move forward instead of holding back.

The naysayers are both outside and inside, and it's hard to fight them—to fight for what you believe in even when you don't always believe it. When I was making my transition out of football, I had one desire. To do something that had never been done before. To create something that had never been created. To build something that hadn't been built. My journey started with that illogical desire and continued with childlike faith. Faith that I could achieve the unreasonable; that I could do the unthinkable. Heck, that I could write a book. I showed up, I did what was in front of me, and I listened not to the doubters, but to the little kid inside of me; the one who always believed. The work was hard, the nights were long, the struggle was real. But it was worth it. Every minute of it.

I ended up returning to the trampoline park a different day. This time, alone, it took me several tries. They were not all pretty, but I finally made the jump. I even stuck the landing. What I was so afraid of never took place. I'm learning to live in the moment and not be afraid of the things that haven't happened yet. Why? Because if I don't there's a chance that they never will.

Be Illogical:

**Sit with your fears, then do it.**
A child lives, breathes, and moves

without fear of the consequences. Logical adults often weigh the legitimate consequences of anything we do. The only life worth living is a life not confined by this fear.

**Focus on what you can do**, not what you think you cannot do.

**Stop weighing the pros and cons and just believe.** Children just believe, they don't overcomplicate things. My coach always used the phrase, "Paralysis by analysis." Don't overthink, just believe, and thus achieve.

You just have to change
your attitude in life
because **YOUR ATTITUDE**
**DETERMINES YOUR**
**ALTITUDE.**

#illogicalbook

# 3

## Don't Forget Your Earmuffs

The year 2019 was the most chaotic year of my life. Particularly the fall. Austin, Texas, was my official home, but I really would've considered myself a nomad. I spent Sunday to Wednesday in Austin, but every Wednesday I would board a 12:00 p.m. flight to New York City. As soon as I would land, my producer would call me, and we would discuss the rundown for the next day's 8:00 a.m. sports show. This call would last for an hour, long enough for me to get in a car and fight the hellacious traffic until I arrived at my hotel. By the time I was settled, it would be 7:00 p.m., giving me just enough time to grab dinner and iron my clothes before that 4:50 a.m. alarm. (Quick life hack: if you're ever too lazy to iron that nice dress or new suit, just hang it up in the bathroom and let the steam from the shower do the work for you.) After Thursday's 8:00 a.m. sports show concluded, I would take a car to Bristol, Connecticut, where I would work Friday and Saturday before ultimately catching a 6:00 a.m. flight back to Austin on Sunday morning. Three different cities, three different states, all within three days. It was chaos.

Nothing brought me greater joy than heading to that airport to go back to Austin Sunday morning, but one November evening, I had to detour. It was a Saturday night and my friend, Tobe Nwigwe, was in town. If you know a thing or two about Nigerians, you know we typically like to stick together and support each other. So rather than head to my much-desired bed after work, I took a car back to New York City.

Tobe is a Nigerian American rapper who was performing at an intimate venue in Manhattan. As I would soon learn, "intimate" and "rap music" are two things that should never mix. I arrived at the concert about an hour early and was escorted backstage to where he and his wife, "Fat" (his affectionate nickname for her, having nothing to do with her size) were rehearsing. Fat, also a rapper, had a toddler at the time, so as she held her baby in one hand, she perused her phone in the other to double-check that she was nailing all her lyrics. "It's show time!" the stage manager yelled as he barged into the room. Everyone grabbed hands to pray in the direction of Tobe. After we bowed our heads and said "Amen," Tobe and Fat proceeded to the stage. I hung back and made my way to a VIP section on the floor.

If you've ever been to a concert, there's nothing like being on the floor right in front of the stage—it's like you're performing with the artist. There's only one small issue with that much proximity. . . . THE MUSIC IS SO LOUD YOU HAVE TO TALK LIKE THIS JUST TO MAKE SURE THE PERSON NEXT TO YOU CAN HEAR! I think I just strained my vocal cords writing that.

The music was so loud, from the subwoofers set in the walls to the speakers on the stage, my ears rang for days after. I stayed for about seven songs, but I needed to leave the concert early because after an hour of being oversaturated by beats, my head was starting to ache on rhythm. I also had to make sure I could catch the redeye back to Austin. Tobe is my friend and all, but remember, my king-size mattress awaited me in my Austin home.

As I was squeezing past clustered bodies toward the exit, I saw a mother holding a child who couldn't have been more than two years old. The child was sound asleep as her mother bobbed left and right clearly feeling the beats from the stage and screaming each of the lyrics as if she were the star of the show. I thought to myself, "How in the world is this child asleep in the midst of all this noise?" I had to find out.

I moved away from the exit and closer toward the mother and child. I figured that at the very least, I could ask the mother for the secret potion that would cause one to rest in that kind of noise. But as I got closer, everything started to make sense. The child was wearing large black earmuffs tucked underneath her hair. She was as calm as could be in the middle of one of the loudest concerts I have ever attended because although there was chaos around her, she was blocking it all out. She decided to put her earmuffs on—or at least someone put them on for her. As I enviously looked on, my ears already starting to ring, I couldn't help but extrapolate this situation to the rest of life.

My lesson that day was: don't forget your earmuffs.

Sometimes our worlds are filled with so much noise that we can't find our way forward. We can't hear our own voice because a million others are screaming what we should do. Logic's voice is especially loud. We need to learn to put on our metaphorical earmuffs so we can walk through the crowd with peace and trust in our own voice. Like the ringing in my ears, that lesson stuck with me for days. In fact, it has not left me even now (the ear ringing is blessedly gone) and it's one I would learn to lean on a few months later when I was met with more noise than I could have ever imagined.

It was minutes before the biggest moment of my career. I was getting ready to record the first-ever episode of *Uncomfortable Conversations with a Black Man*, the show that would ultimately change my life and lead me to connecting with Oprah. I had arrived at the studio for my 11:00 a.m. call time. I reached out to open the door when all of a sudden, my phone vibrated. I was so on edge about the big day that the sudden vibrations sent my nerves out of control. The text message I received was from a black friend and colleague at ESPN. I had run the idea of the show by her days before, back when the title was *Questions White People Have* (I know, I like the final title better, too). I was met with a little hesitancy, but ultimately, she listened to my heart and offered me some advice in the moment.

The text got straight to the point: "I know I mentioned this already, but maybe hold off on your 'White People Ask Questions'—I don't think that's the way."

Truly, it was too late. I quickly typed a response back. "If you got another way, let me know as soon as possible? I'm going to move how God leads, but I will keep you updated." There was no turning back now—I had rented a room, hired a videographer, and spent hours preparing to tackle one of America's biggest issues: racism. Yet my friend texted me this message four minutes before I was supposed to record. It sent me spiraling into a roller coaster of doubt. "What if I fail? What if I embarrass myself?" I thought. Those same fear-based questions I had while stuck on the trampoline were beginning to creep in again, but this wasn't just a backflip.

Admittedly, I was frustrated. I didn't understand why a close friend of mine would cast doubt on something that I felt called to do. She wasn't involved, so it didn't make sense to me why she cared so much about my plans, and why she was so against them. I continued to question myself, but time was running out. I had a decision to make. Either listen to her doubts, or put my earmuffs on. After a few minutes of internal deliberation, I chose the latter. I texted my friend back again and told her we could discuss over the phone after I finished recording. Minutes later, I sat down in my chair, opened my mouth, and let the words flow out. Eighty million views across social media platforms and a number-one *New York Times* bestselling book later, I'm glad I made that decision. I'm glad I put my earmuffs on.

When you are called to do something great, either by someone else or by your own internal yearning, there are always plenty of skeptics. Skeptics may pop up in the form of haters or they might be well-meaning friends who disagree, like my friend. Regardless, **your calling is *your* calling. It's not a conference call**. Only you know that pure passion that burns within you. Only you know how many hours you've laid awake at night just thinking, "What if? What if I start that business? What if I pursue that relationship? What if I move to that city?" The "what-ifs" are endless, but so, too, is the noise. It's hard to shut it out, to make the decision to put on your earmuffs, but without them we can never truly listen to ourselves and find our truest path. That is why it is imperative you put on your earmuffs. Your earmuffs don't keep the doubt from existing, they keep the external noise from impacting your existence.

When I made the decision to ignore my friend's cautionary text message, I did what I believed to be right. Was it illogical? Absolutely. I was a former NFL player turned sports analyst about to sit in an all-white room talking to myself on camera about one of the most divisive and important topics in the country. I was putting myself smack dab in the center of our nation's biggest source of tension. By being illogical, I made a decision to disregard the doubt. A decision to believe. A decision to chase my dream. Who would have thought that by chasing an illogical dream I would be able to influence people for the better?

I'm not saying that we shouldn't seek the counsel of others, but we can learn to choose when to engage and when to put our heads down and move forward. My favorite example of this is Apple's latest earphones, the AirPods Pro. They come with a nifty new noise cancellation feature. The AirPods Pro allow you to fully cancel all of the sound around you to the point where you can't even hear yourself speak. You can only hear whatever sound you've decided to play through your earphones. The noise cancellation is handy, but what I find even more impressive is a different feature called the transparency function. At the press of a button, noise cancellation is turned off. This allows you to hear enough outside noise to engage in a conversation with someone while still listening to your music. You now have complete control of the noise you let in, and also control of when you want to silence outside noise. Not all noise is bad noise. Not everyone who challenges your ideas or your ability is doubting you—some of their feedback can be constructive. Understand when you need to completely block out the noise or when it's beneficial to engage in constructive dialogue. Sometimes learning to put on your earmuffs is as simple as acknowledging the criticism in your mind but not letting it overwhelm you or change your course. Almost like saying, "Hey, I see you, but stay over there." Each time the noise gets quieter and quieter, and your earmuffs get stronger as you get stronger. If we are aware but not overwhelmed, sometimes we can even let something good slip in.

Before *Uncomfortable Conversations*, I had already received my fair share of criticism on social media. Whether they were Twitter bots or human beings, people didn't always like what I had to say. Threats and hateful, hurtful remarks had been thrown at me long before my videos went viral. I knew I was speaking truth and mastering my craft, but as I got better, the comments got worse. Still, I stayed the course. When I first began posting videos tackling issues of race, the hate I received intensified. That's how I knew I was close. I didn't back down; I refused to run away. Breath by breath, the doubters' sting began to dissipate. I blocked out that noise and it set me free.

A year later, I was under fire again, but this time for a different issue. Being targeted on social media is similar to being the brunt of the jokes in your favorite group chat, except the jokes never end, the chat is limitless, and whoever wants to join has free access. It's like being the candy-filled piñata at a child's birthday—first the kids take a few swings, but eventually the adults pick up the bat and swing until they break you.

I was under attack for my comments on America upholding its suspension of sprinter Sha'Carri Richardson, who tested positive for marijuana and was kept out of the 2021 Olympic Games in Tokyo. "A rule is a rule," I said. "Competing under the influence of THC [the active compound found in marijuana] may be okay for the Olympic sprinter who runs in a straight line, but what about the javelin thrower?" I wasn't sure why this comment was garnering so much hate, but after roughly ten thousand different individuals scorned me across multiple platforms, I decided to do some research. Full transparency: I've never smoked weed. So I am ignorant of the impact from a personal level, and I also was not fully aware of the history of racism around marijuana. The social media hate was loud and it was layered. Many people just wanted to attack me because it's easy to do when you can remain relatively anonymous. But amidst all the noise, there was a doctor named Benecia Williams who made a comment of her own. Her message to me was simple: "Look up Harry Anslinger." I had my earmuffs on but I decided to let this through. She and I began to engage, and it turned out she is a double-board-certified physician who specializes in rehabilitation. She is a huge advocate of the positive impact CBD (a non-psychoactive drug found in the cannabis plant) can have on one's health.

I followed her request and started looking up Harry Anslinger. It turns out he was the first head of the Federal Bureau of Narcotics. In the 1930s, Anslinger pushed to have marijuana outlawed in America, but for many wrong reasons. He was once quoted as saying, "Reefer makes darkies think they're as good as white men." He also said, "There are 100,000 total marijuana smokers in the U.S., and most are Negroes, Hispanics, Filipinos, and entertainers. Their Satanic music, jazz and swing, results from marijuana usage. This marijuana causes white women to seek sexual relations with Negroes, entertainers, and any others." Anslinger created what was called the "gore files," roughly two hundred accounts of the most heinous sexually and physically violent crimes committed in the country. He would alter these files and attribute the crimes to the usage of marijuana. That is how he pushed the fear of marijuana from the state level to the national level. He ultimately used these files to convince Congress to pass the Marihuana Tax Act of 1937, outlawing the use of marijuana.

The only reason I learned all of this information and grew intellectually was because I was willing to let some positive noise in. Among the thousands of disparaging comments I blocked out, there was absolutely something worth listening to—one comment that made me better informed and strengthened me as a person, instead of tearing me down as noise often does.

But another question remains: What happens when you're the one who's doubting yourself? What happens when the doubts won't go away? At that moment, it's time to sign an eviction notice. Here's what I mean: Many people will try to guide you, convince you, doubt you, or direct you. Their opinions and thoughts of you may have made their way deep into the crevices of your mind and heart and seemingly set up camp there. They're cozy. Nuzzled in and comfortably living inside of you in spaces that, quite frankly, are not meant for them. How and when they arrived was their fault. But now, it's time to take control of the situation. It's time to kick them out. The fear has been living rent-free and the bills are past due. It's time for some new friends, new opinions, and new beliefs about yourself.

My friend's cautionary text message may have been rooted in fear. Maybe she was afraid that I wasn't ready for the ridicule, the comments, the weight my words would carry. Whatever her reasons, I had to put my earmuffs on. As you begin your own journey of being illogical, remember: Not everyone is going to cheer you on. Even fewer people are going to want to see you succeed. They may be insecure, frustrated, or even confused. That's okay. Be illogical and go for it anyway. Your dream is not meant to be hidden.

The thing that sets people apart in life is what they actually believe about themselves. Deep down in their heart of hearts, in the depths of their soul. Do you believe that you can change the world? Do you believe you can do something that's never been done before? Do you believe that you can free yourself from logic's limits and start living life differently? Do you believe that you can live a life free from fear of failure? Many times, when we hear questions like these, they're asked with cynicism, as if considering such things is a waste of time and energy—that you'd have to be foolish to believe in something so unbelievable. Hear me when I say this: I want you to be dumb enough to believe.

I actually believed I could change the world with one video. I actually believed I was the perfect person to tackle race-related issues in America and around the world. I still do. I believe that I was made for this moment. Why? Because I have been preparing for it my whole life. The night before the first filming, I made a phone call. I called my brother, Sam, and made a statement that I still believe to this day.

"Bro," I began, "I don't know how to explain it, but I think I was made for this moment. My upbringing, my relationships, my background, and my life experiences. I don't know anyone better suited to answer some of these questions from our white brothers and sisters than me. Something has to be done, and I think I'm the person to do it."

I had a feeling. I believed . . . and sure, some would call me dumb for believing, but what if I hadn't gone forward anyway? I don't want to imagine everything I would have missed out on for the sake of staying in my lane, thinking logically, and leaving this important work to someone else. I was crazy enough to believe. Are you?

About a year later, I went to another one of Tobe's concerts. This time, I came prepared. I had some bright yellow earmuffs to match my banana-colored jacket. But I wasn't the only one. Tobe's daughter was there as well—with her own earmuffs on. Just a bit older, she was nuzzled quietly in her mother's arms. When I saw her, I asked Fat if I could carry her. She said yes. So I picked up the child and rocked her to sleep in the midst of a loud rap concert.

Be Illogical:

**Don't listen to the haters.** Don't let others' doubts limit your achievement.

**Not all noise is bad noise.** Activate your transparency function and let the good in to refine you while keeping out the bad.

**Sign the eviction notice.** Kick out your own internal negative thoughts whenever they arise.

# YOUR CALLING IS YOUR CALLING.

## It's not a conference call.

# 4

---

# Keep on Dreaming

In the end, reconciliation is a spiritual process, which requires more
than just a legal framework. It has
to happen in the hearts and minds
of people.

—NELSON MANDELA

What happens when you can't put on your earmuffs? When the words of the doubters are too
loud and get in anyway? The answer is found in the
story of Joseph.

Joseph was a dreamer. The second youngest of twelve siblings, he was hands down his father's favorite child. Joseph's dad even made him a custom colorful coat—think limited edition Chanel or the freshest Jordans—to show how much he loved him. He was the golden boy, but he had a peculiar talent. A talent that would save his life, but also put him in grave danger.

One night, Joseph had a dream that all of his brothers and his dad were bowing down to him. He shared that dream with his brothers. They were livid. (Quick aside, if you ever have a dream that your siblings are bowing down to you, you should probably keep that one to yourself.) Shortly after, Joseph had another dream. This time he dreamed that the sun, the moon, and eleven stars were bowing down to him, as well.

Joseph's older brothers were sick of their father's favoritism and tired of their baby brother's dreams, so they decided to get rid of him. They sold him into Egyptian slavery and sent him off to Egypt. Joseph ended up in an Egyptian prison, where he became known for his ability to interpret dreams. He wowed the other inmates, and they remembered him even after they were released.

Twelve years passed when Pharaoh, the king of Egypt, had two dreams that no one could interpret. In fact, he was so disturbed by the dreams that he summoned all of Egypt's magicians and their wise men to see if they could make sense of them. No luck. Now, what Pharaoh wants, Pharaoh gets. So while the magicians and wise men did not have the ability to interpret the dreams, they believed there had to be someone who could. One day, one of the king's aides remembered Joseph from years prior when he'd been in prison with him. Joseph was summoned from prison to the king's court, interpreted Pharaoh's dream, and, as a reward, was made second in command over all of Egypt. Pharaoh went as far as to say, "Only in the throne will I be greater than you" (Genesis 41:40).

Think about that for a second. Joseph, whose dreams caused his brothers to despise him, so much so that they left him for dead, also led him to being second in command over the most powerful country of the time. This story, this lesson, stops me in my tracks every time I read it. Remember, along your journey toward being illogical, people will doubt you, ridicule you, gossip about you, and maybe even leave you in an emotional ditch. We try to put on our earmuffs, but sometimes it's too much. Just know it will all come full circle. The same things that people despised you for will lead you to your destiny.

The very thing that people, his own brothers included, hated him for was the same thing that placed Joseph second in command. When people shun you in life for your dreams, just keep on dreaming.

When Joseph interpreted Pharaoh's dream, he told the king that the dream meant the land of Egypt would face seven years of harvest followed by seven years of famine. The king took heed of Joseph's words and immediately began to store up and ration all the grain, allocating it daily in preparation for the years to come. Neighboring countries and communities were dependent upon Egypt, so the king had to plan accordingly. One day, Joseph's brothers left the town where they were living, a town experiencing great famine, and went to Egypt to buy grain. Joseph was now the governor of the land and was the one in charge of selling grain to foreigners who came to purchase it from Egypt. I'm sure you can tell where this story is going. As Joseph's brothers came forward, he recognized them, but they did not recognize him. It had been twelve years, and the customs of Egypt at the time likely called for Joseph to have a shaved head. As they drew near to Joseph,

Egyptian royalty, they bowed their heads to the ground. In that moment, Joseph's dream from years before came true. His brothers had no idea who he was—they probably thought their brother was still in slavery or dead somewhere. He wasn't. Joseph was about to bless his brothers, the same brothers who punished him. After his brothers retook their positions standing upright, they purchased the grain and were sent on their way back home. But as they arrived home, they realized that not only did they have the grain they went to purchase, but Joseph had also put the money they were supposed to use to purchase the grain back in their sacks.

Before I created my video series I had already envisioned a book, *Uncomfortable Conversations with a Black Man*. I felt as though the spoken word has sizzle, but the written word has substance. The only problem was that I didn't know anything about writing books, so I reached out to my literary agent. I expressed my idea, how I wanted each chapter to start off with a question that was then answered throughout the chapter. How I wanted the book to be conversational; I wanted to talk with the reader, not at the reader. I poured out my idea with excitement, but the excitement wasn't reciprocated. I was met with comments about the market being too saturated and ears not being very keen on this type of subject matter. I was disheartened. I had a calling and I believed the world was ready to listen. I had a decision to make: listen to the experts, or go with the command of my calling. Well, by now you know which decision I made.

I'll be honest, even after the book was published I was still bitter. I harbored resentment that people had doubted me, that people hadn't believed in me. But then I remembered Joseph. After you've made the illogical decision, you'll likely have a moment when you think back on those who doubted you. Make sure you think of them fondly, because everything happened as it was supposed to. It always does. That relationship that ended, that business partner that abandoned you, that bank that would not give you a loan, it happened exactly how it needed to happen. It will all work out for your good.

Before *Uncomfortable Conversations with a Black Man*, before the views, before the likes, before *The Bachelor*, my dream was to make art. I wanted to do something that's never been done before. I would come early, stay late, wear my earmuffs, and jump out of boats (more on this in future chapters). People thought I was crazy, but the dam broke and I started using my "it," (more on finding and using your "it" in chapter 15). I could feel myself in the zone. Maximizing my potential and leaving the world better for it. I was still at ESPN and was hoping to grow at the worldwide television leader. And then I met a roadblock. As I was negotiating for an increased role with the company, one of the decision makers looked me in the eye and told me that what I was trying to do couldn't be done. She told me that I wasn't a big enough name. So I left, and went to a company that allowed me more space to grow. I made an illogical decision. Then, weeks later, my platform did grow; far bigger than any show or network could have ever expected. They thought that the sky was the limit. I knew that logic was. So I made an illogical decision and bet on myself. I took a risk.

After Joseph became second in command, a famine hit and there would be limited food in the land. His brothers, who figured he was dead by then, traveled to Egypt to get food for their family. They ran into Joseph but again, they didn't recognize him. It had been over twenty years since they sold him into slavery. Joseph recognized them instantly, and though he could have harbored hate in his heart, he forgave them and gave them food to eat and a place to stay. Even when they don't believe in your dreams, bless them anyway.

I'm not mad at the executive at ESPN. I have no qualms about my book agent, nor the colleague who said that *Uncomfortable Conversations* was a bad idea. I have no issues with anyone who has been limited by logic. I actually wrote this book for them. Regardless of what you've experienced in life, I can tell you this much. **Where you're going is greater than where you've been.** I wrote this book for you. For all those who feel like there must be something more. If you've ever felt like there must be something more, that's because there is. If you've ever felt limited by life, that probably means you have been, but those days are over. You no longer need to cling to a faint hope—you have all the steps to take action. I've heard a definition of "faith" described as: "the substance of things hoped for, the evidence of things unseen." Faith is only necessary as long as there is doubt, but eventually your faith will be your eyes. You no longer need to have faith that your dreams, hopes, and ambitions will come true. You have all the tools to make them come true and let your faith become your eyes. You no longer have to imagine a life without failure; just go live one. Anyone who has ever felt limited by life. For people who once believed that they could change the world, then stopped believing. That's why I do what I do. I didn't choose *Uncomfortable Conversations*; *Uncomfortable Conversations* chose me. My preparation, desire to make an impact, and belief that anything is possible as long as you believe was what prepared me for my moment. You're not too smart for own good, but you have been limiting yourself with logic. My intention is to unlock your potential, and to rid you of the bitterness and hate before they take root in you. But I had to learn not to harbor hate the hard way.

I was a junior in high school and could not have been more excited to receive my first offer to play football at the University of Texas. The premier school in the state and a top school in the nation, Texas was big. And my high school was small. And small schools sometimes keep people from dreaming.

I was walking out of science class when he said it. "Hey, Emmanuel," this professor began, "are you sure you want to go to Texas? I don't think you're going to survive there. It's too big, and you're from a small school. You'll probably get lost in the shuffle. Why don't you reconsider?" Maybe this teacher was having a bad day or maybe he just genuinely disliked me (I didn't like him very much after that either), but those words hurt. And I carried them with me. I couldn't wait to prove him wrong. But even after I achieved success in both college and the NFL, I was still angry. I would come back to campus just to ignore him. I would make sure to call him out during interviews. Anger is a secondary emotion, meaning that there's something else beneath it that we truly feel. The thing beneath anger for me was sadness. I was sad that this person close to me would be so negative; would doubt me without even giving me a chance. Sadness led to anger, and anger hate. But then I remembered a quote about love and hatred from Martin Luther King Jr.: "Hate cannot drive out hate; only love can do that." I resolved to love and forgive this man, and everyone else who didn't believe. Don't get me wrong, we weren't best of friends afterward, but that hate fell off of my heart and I was free to be me. Free to serve all, not just some. And that freedom is what allowed my light to shine.

I don't know what you've been through in life,

but hatred and resentment are never the answer. They never were. When you start being illogical and proving doubters wrong, don't say, "I told you so," just smile and say, "Thank you. Thank you for making me uncomfortable. Thank you for pushing me. Thank you for the doubt. Thank you for helping me devote my life to proving you wrong." As illogical as it sounds, doubters can be great motivators. Maybe these naysayers just need somebody to show them that the impossible can be done. That they can be free, too. And who knows, there may just be a famine in town and you might end up as second in command with the power to help.

Joseph had a dream, literally. But you too will have a dream for your life. Dreams of where you want to go, what you want to do, what you want to accomplish. You've probably already experienced this already, but some will despise you simply because of your dreams. Your ambition will cause their envy. Your success will lead to their hate. Those in your corner and those closest to you will doubt or discourage you. But hear me when I say this. Just keep on dreaming. Eventually everything they doubted will be in high demand. Their hate will turn into high praise. And what they envied you for, you will excel in.

Be Illogical:

**When people shun you in life for your dreams, keep on dreaming.** When we release ourselves of logic, it may seem like we're traveling further from our destination, but like the boomerang, everything comes full circle. I went from going to detention for talking to being asked to speak to Fortune 500 companies. Your gifts will eventually make room for you. As an adolescent I was far from the brightest student at my elite college preparatory school, St. Mark's. I graduated toward the bottom of the class and I often got sent to detention for talking too much. So you'll understand how ironic I found it when I received a call to deliver the opening convocation speech for St. Mark's. I've also won two Emmys for the talking that I do. The very thing I got punished for doing years earlier, I was now being asked to do; I was being rewarded for it. Joseph had a similar story and I trust you will, too.

**Don't blame the haters.** Our brains are prewired with fear sensors. They help protect us from danger, but also limit us from achieving the impossible. Not everyone will have the same passion or fervor for greatness that you carry. Don't blame them. Bitterness can erode your soul.

**Don't harbor hate.** One of my biggest struggles in life is navigating the pain of my past. Those who doubted me, questioned me, and downright wished ill toward me. We all know those people who never wanted you to succeed, and in fact did everything within their power to keep you from succeeding. Maybe it was a coach, teacher, friend, or even parent. It wasn't until recently that I realized that resentment was only having adverse effects on my life. I learned not to harbor hate.

# WHERE YOU'RE GOING
## IS GREATER
### than where you've been.

 #illogicalbook

# 5

---

# I Might Be Crazy

In 2013, I had just been traded to the Philadelphia Eagles from the Browns. Trades in the NFL are rare and though I was a bit surprised, I was happy to be leaving Cleveland. The franchise had been struggling for nearly two decades with no sign of getting better. After a losing record and a gruesome injury (I tore a ligament in my knee), I got the call that I was headed to a new city, with a new coach and a new opportunity. I was going to Philly.

It was late May when I walked up the steps of the Eagles' facility to meet the special teams coach, Dave Fipp. I wanted to get some extra film study in with him, but I had also learned the tricks of the NFL. If you want to make the roster as someone in my position who is low in the pecking order, the special teams coach better become your best friend.

While sitting with the coach reviewing practice tape, I glanced to the right and noticed what appeared to be an updated depth chart. A depth chart is a list of every player on the roster in order of their importance, based on position. When my eyes saw the label "Linebackers," I worked down the list of names to find my own. Except I never did. I scanned the list again—nothing. The coach was still talking me through corrections but I was no longer able to pay attention. I sat there trying to play it cool. I finally found my name under a small label at the bottom of the board that read "Cut." Cut is a term used in the NFL for when a team is going to release, fire, or relieve you of your duties, rendering you jobless. My name was on that list along with three other individuals. Four names, three letters, two options: believe it or don't.

I dismissed myself from the meeting and didn't

bother to offer an explanation. I needed a minute, desperate for solitude to gather my thoughts and pray. After pacing back and forth down the hall, I realized there was one place I could go to be alone. You guessed it—I made a beeline to the bathroom. Ducking into the far stall, I locked the door and got down on one knee to pray. Not the most sanitary thing I've ever done, but the thought of being cut by a team that had just traded for me would drive any young man crazy. I knew what my eyes had seen, that I was to be released, but I refused to believe— and more important, accept—it. I was on hands and knees in a full plea to God that somehow things would turn. After all, regardless of what the chart said about my future, I was still currently employed. Mid-prayer, I cracked an eye open to see pants folding around someone's feet in the stall next to me and realized I was no longer by myself. I knelt there with tears in my eyes, with a stranger in the stall next to me, feeling completely alone. It was then I thought to myself, "I might be crazy."

I'm going to level with you. Full transparency. There will be a moment on your illogical journey to-ward truth when you say to yourself, "What the heck am I doing?" Or more likely, "I might be crazy!" Let me be the first to tell you that that feeling is okay. I'm pretty sure the person who first thought, "Ya know, we should go to space," probably thought shortly thereafter, "Eh, maybe not, that's crazy." **The moment you think to yourself, "I might be crazy," is the first checkpoint on your path to accomplishing greatness**. When you have that moment, don't lean into your doubt. Let it propel you to the reality that you are about to do something great. Your "I might be crazy" moment may come when you start to empty your bank account to pursue the business that will change your life. It may come when you end that five-year relationship that everyone—including you—thought would result in marriage. It may come when you sell your possessions and move overseas to help people in need. Whatever it is, it's coming. Embrace it.

In 2007, the iPhone was released. But first, Steve Jobs had a vision. You see, he had this idea—a crazy idea, may I add—that we could hold in our hand a device that would act as a telephone, camera, music player, and GPS system all in one. When Jobs decided to create the iPhone, many thought it was a ridiculous idea and that he had no business trying to revolutionize anything. That things were fine the way they were and that his product wouldn't work. Most doubted, but others believed. He was one of the believers. His belief was so strong that he transferred that same belief to his employees, the people who moved house and home to follow him, the people who worked harder than they ever had before to help him accomplish his vision. Bob Iger, the former CEO of the Walt Disney Company, had heard of Jobs's idea to create a device that could hold music and videos and partnered with him to find ways to deliver more Disney content to the masses. Who wouldn't want more Mickey Mouse in their life?

Fifteen years after an "I might be crazy" moment could have ended it all, the dream Jobs wouldn't let go of has led to more than 1 billion sales worldwide. (The iPhone is the most purchased phone in history and has completely changed the way the world works. All because one man believed and did it anyway.)

Jobs didn't keep his faith to himself; he spread it. When you're unwaveringly illogical, others catch on and start to be illogical with you. Your "I might be crazy" moment is a minor speed bump to keep you honest. Realistically, it's there to slow you down, but you don't drive up to a speed bump, look at it, then turn around and go in the other direction. You plow over the speed bump because you have somewhere to be or, if you're like me, you check to see if there are any cars coming and you go around it—got to make sure I keep the shocks on my car protected. Your "I might be crazy" moment is a sign that you're alive. Remember that what you're trying to accomplish isn't normal, and that your brain will try to remind you of the limitations it has adopted from society over time. Ignore them. Believe in yourself, and eventually people will begin to believe in you, too.

Exactly two weeks after my bathroom stall moment, I was still on the roster but two of the players on that list were already gone and the third was cut that day. He had gone early to the team barbecue and texted me the news when he found out. I didn't know what to do. This was our last team bonding event before we went away for a quick summer break and then came back for training camp. What was supposed to be a fun get-together was now fair game for my release. I went anyway. Full of fear but determined, I showed up, checked in with my coaches, did my mingling duties, and left.

My phone never rang. I wasn't released.

Those weeks were two of the most difficult weeks

of my life. Though I was working and believing, the burden of the unknown still weighed on me heavily. It got worse when I saw my teammates get cut. With each call, with each decision, my perceived reality became that much more real. The day I walked into that meeting room and saw the depth chart, I had been tempted to call the other players and tell them what I had seen. But that wasn't my job, and I didn't want them to experience the pain I was experiencing. My job—my only job—was to believe the unbelievable. To put hope in the unseen.

The cards hadn't been flipped; the decision hadn't been rendered. I decided to walk by faith, not by sight. I decided to hope, even when hope didn't seem like an option. I went on to make the team and start the majority of games that year.

On any given day, we make judgments about ourselves and our situations based on what we see and believe. Then, we default to logic. We fall back on what's comfortable. We want things to get better immediately, and if they don't, we lose hope. But the fact is, things may get worse before they get better. Even if they do, believe anyway. Dreams aren't linear. People will be cut, your doubts will seem more real, your fears may even grow. Stay the course. Your own journey will not be easy, but I promise you: It will be worth it. Worth the time, the friendships, the risk. Logic limits. There is more to be seen. Your journey is not over. It's just beginning.

A few months later, I found myself back in Coach Fipp's office, this time to game plan for our season opener against Detroit. I looked up at the depth chart and saw my name right where it belonged, underneath the "Captains" header. After playing well on defense and helping lead our team to a strong season, I was starting on special teams and many of my fellow players looked to me for leadership. I would be voted First Team All-Pro, Special Teams—the best at my position in the entirety of the NFL—by Pro Football Focus.

What I came to realize from the first meeting to the next, from one moment to another, was that I wasn't actually crazy.

> You see, when you say a phrase like, "I might be crazy," you have to remember "might" is the operative word. **I was perfectly sane, but I was dangerously illogical.**

I played three more seasons for the Eagles. And though I left the team before they won their first

Super Bowl, I was a part of the core that built the culture there. I taught people how to be illogical. To challenge the status quo. Teammates, coaches, and staff began living life illogically without fear of failure. They believed that they, with a first-time head coach, a second-year quarterback, and no Super Bowl wins, could triumph in the most celebrated game in all of sport. They believed that a backup quarterback, a man who had been cut many times before, could lead them to a championship after their starter got hurt. People called us crazy, but we were just illogical.

My whole life has been full of "I might be crazy" moments. Making the team, going from cut to captain, having uncomfortable conversations, and hosting my own television show—all before the age of thirty. When you're illogical, you'll have your "I might be crazy" moment too, but it's just a moment. A speed bump you are meant to cross. Yes, you *might* be crazy, but you also *might not* be. You might be perfectly sane, perfectly in your right mind, perfectly illogical.

Be Illogical:

**Believe yourself, not your eyes.** When you're illogical, sometimes you literally can't believe your eyes. Through weeks of tirelessly working and believing, I reversed the reality of the word "cut" that I'd read and kept my spot on the team.

**Get comfortable in uncomfortable situations.** I promise, when you believe in the impossible, you will end up in some very peculiar situations and surroundings. When I found myself in the bathroom stall of an NFL facility, I did not freak out. I sat down, took my backpack off, and I got comfortable. Only then did the path forward become clear.

**"Crazy" is a speed bump, not a roadblock.** When you find yourself stuck in a mess, keep inching forward. Slowing down can allow you to see the best way forward, but don't stop.

**When things get grim, hope.** As each player on the cut list was released, things began to look even more grim

for me. But I continued to cling to even
the slightest possibility I would make
it through. Along your journey, when
trying to achieve the unthinkable, it
will get worse before it gets better. Hope
anyway.

The moment you think
to yourself, **"I MIGHT
BE CRAZY,"** is the first
checkpoint on your path to
accomplishing greatness.

# 6

## The Battle Line

When the Philistine arose and drew
near to meet David, David ran
quickly toward the battle line to
meet the Philistine.

—1 SAMUEL 17:48

Most people have heard the story of David and Goliath, but allow me to remind you. David was a
young Israelite boy, the youngest of all his siblings.
His daily life consisted of herding sheep and playing

a musical instrument called a lyre for the king. Insert Goliath, a Philistine giant who stood nine feet, nine inches tall, a smidge below a basketball hoop. And boy, did he have the confidence and attitude to match his size. He had a vulgar mouth and talked more trash than the drunk frat guy who is always looking to get into a fight.

Goliath was set to fight one Israelite in a winner-take-all battle. Think of it like a UFC championship fight, but without a referee to stop the match from becoming deadly. Rather than win a championship belt, the loser's nation would become slaves to the winner's. This was going to be a monumental matchup. The only issue? All of Israel's soldiers backed down. I would too if a nine-foot-nine, trash-talking frat guy—I mean, Goliath—challenged me. But then there was David.

A shepherd, David was a warrior at heart. Without realizing it, he had been preparing for this battle his whole life. His duties as a shepherd meant he hunted animals who stole sheep from the flock, killing lions and bears if they tried to kill him first.

Being a shepherd was seen as a mundane job. Taking care of sheep didn't require the skill or courage necessary to go to war—anyone could do it. Or so people thought. As the youngest of his brothers and neither tall nor physically intimidating, David was relegated to this role. His family figured that he was best suited to staying at home watching the sheep, while his older, more "courageous" brothers joined the men in Israel's army.

Quick aside, there will be times when people look down on you for one reason or another, maybe because of your size, your stature, your age, your race, your gender, or your beliefs. Don't listen to them. Maybe you don't like where you are in life right now, but it may be exactly where you've needed to be in order to prepare you and catapult you toward your destiny. Work hard at the job in front of you. Put the time in. Be the best shepherd that the world has ever seen. Refine your skills. Tend to your sheep. Other shepherds may be asleep, thinking that this idle time is a waste of time. Don't worry about them. Fight lions. Master your craft.

No matter where you're at, people may look down upon you. They may devalue you or underestimate your ability. Let them. It's not your job to explain to them why they're wrong. Your job is to show up, each and every day. To face the giants in your life, even when everyone else is afraid.

An entire army was afraid of a nine-foot-nine giant. But David wasn't. David showed up to battle by accident. He was at home with his pops, watching the sheep. But with three sons fighting in the war, David's father, Jesse, grew concerned. He asked David to go check on his brothers and deliver them some food. (I guess Uber Eats isn't all that new.) As soon as David made it to the front lines, he heard Goliath's shouts of arrogance. The giant was taunting the Israelites, asking who would be brave enough to battle him. No one was willing to face him. Except David.

In combat, a battle line is a line defining the positions of opposing groups. It's where ownership is taken and it can dictate the fate of what is to come. When you're illogical, you first have to win the war within your own mind. You have to defeat the negative thoughts and trust that it will work out even when it looks ugly. You have to believe you can defeat the giant. Remember that you already have all the necessary tools to be the greatest version of yourself. This is your moment. If you want to win the war, you have to face your battles head-on. Now, you just have to step up to the battle line.

After some of the best trash talk that would surely be censored on today's television, David was ready to fight Goliath. Remember, whoever won this battle would save their people from slavery. Whoever lost would put their people into subjugation. I can hear it now: "*Let's get ready to ruuuuuumble!*" David wasted no time.

"Then it happened when the Philistine rose and came and drew near to meet David, that David ran quickly toward the battle line to meet the Philistine. And David put his hand into his bag and took from it a stone and slung it, and struck the Philistine in his forehead. And the stone sank into his forehead, so that he fell on his face to the ground." (1 Samuel 17:48–53). The battle was won and the enemy was defeated, all because David wasn't afraid to approach the line head-on.

The most important part is that "David ran quickly toward the battle line to meet the Philistine." Okay, y'all, picture this. The nine-foot-nine giant, the biggest bully in all the land, starts sprinting toward you. What's your move? Let me tell you what I'm *not* doing—I'm not charging directly at him. I'm turning around, dropping all my belongings, and running in the other direction while screaming for help and simultaneously trying to hail a taxi. But not David. He ran toward the battle line—toward the opponent. This is how illogical you and I need to be, because this kind of illogical courage is what it will take to slay the Goliaths in our lives. Whether people or your own doubts and insecurities, meet your Goliaths head-on and win that war at the battle line.

For many of us, our Goliath is quite literally our fear, or the fear other people impose on us. We all have different fears. But **don't let other people's fears become your own**. I'll say it again: do not let other people's fears become your own. For example, mortuusequusphobia is the fear of ketchup. I swear it's a real thing. When I was in the fifth grade, I went to my close friend John's house. We were chilling around the table eating a burger when all of a sudden, he ran behind the couch screaming. His older brother, George, was in high school and had just walked inside and hurled something our way. I didn't flinch; whatever he chucked seemed harmless. As the object landed on the table, I confirmed my suspicions. It was harmless. At least to me it was. It was a plastic ketchup packet. I picked it up and looked at it, and wondered what in the world had sent John sprinting away. After George saw his brother's initial reaction, his inner big-brother bully came out and he continued hurling packets at John. John hid behind the chair for another five minutes. I was confused; I never asked John about the incident because I didn't want to embarrass him, but later I learned he had mortuusequusphobia. He had a fear of ketchup.

While John couldn't finish the rest of his burger, and he lost his appetite for the fries, I simply bent down, grabbed a couple of ketchup packets off the floor, tore them open, and continued munching (after checking on him, of course). I wasn't going to let his fear influence me; I wasn't going to be afraid of his fear. David wasn't afraid of the same giant that all of Israel was afraid of. He thought to himself, "Just because you're scared doesn't mean I have to be." Others will be afraid of your dreams. Others will think they're impossible, too risky, too dangerous. They may have been scared to start that business or end that relationship; to change careers or change course. Don't let their fear impact you; their fear is theirs.

The first time I watched the video of the murder of George Floyd, my heart sank. I was devastated. During the previous football season just a few months before, I had heard an outcry of rage from white sports aficionados who watched Myles Garrett, a black player in the NFL, swing his helmet toward Mason Rudolph, a white player. You could feel their anger; you could cut it with a knife. But now, after the murder of an unarmed black man at the hands of a white police officer, I heard nothing. I felt sick. Confused. Guilty. My whole career was still centered on football at the time, but I had to do something. I wanted to speak to sports fans but I knew they weren't coming to my page to hear about social issues.

Still, I had to speak out. I, and many other people around me, had been cautioned for years about taking on racism in the public eye and losing our platforms by going political. People didn't think it was a good time to have an uncomfortable conversation. Many believed that the subject matter was too complex, that it wasn't the right place. That I wasn't the right person. I didn't listen to them. Minutes after watching and processing my emotions, I sat in my chair, turned on my camera, and shared my heart with the world. This video would be different from any other I had ever done. I wasn't talking about sports or championships; I was confronting racism and hatred. Anytime I addressed issues of race on social media, much of my audience would leave. They would scroll past the tweets and wait for me to post about football. But the pain that I was experiencing was too deep to hold in. God was beginning to show me that my calling would be much bigger than any Super Bowl championship or sporting event. I would be tackling issues that led to the deaths of innocent people; issues that people avoided for as long as I could remember. I was not afraid—but others were. I had been shepherding conversations like these for years now, at times within my friend group and at other times within my city. After Colin Kaepernick first took a knee, I brought together the Austin, Texas, police chief and some influencers for a conversation that was broadcast locally. I had already attempted to slay the lions in my life, but now it was time to take on the Goliath of racism. I refused to let the fears and cautionary tales of others stop me. Run to the battle line; too much is at stake.

There's a final thing I'd like to note about David's fight with Goliath. He chose to fight with a stone and a sling. No breastplate, no sword. He tried to wear a bronze helmet and a coat of armor, but he couldn't move. He stripped them off and fought as he knew how. On your illogical journey toward find-ing your truth, this is key. Fight the way you know how. If you're a lover, love. If you're calm, use peace. If you're loud and bold, use it. The tools you bring to the table are more than enough. What slings do you have? What battles have you won? Use what you have. Now is not the time to change your tactics; remember who you are. David, at his core, was a shepherd, trained intensively in protecting sheep from wild animals. I, at my core, am a communica-tor. In my fight against systemic racism, never once did I protest. I haven't marched, I haven't held up a sign. It didn't fit me. What did fit me was speak-ing out and using my words to dismantle oppres-sion. My words were my weapons, nothing else. You don't need to fight like anyone else. But you do need to fight. You need to run; you need to sprint to the battle line.

You may be someone who is afraid of confronta-tion. You may tense up at the idea of letting some-one down. You may get stressed out at the *idea* of an uncomfortable conversation. Doubt your doubts. Ignore your fears. Drop your sword and pick up your sling. Find a stone. People often ask, "What's the worst that could happen?" Maybe you lose a friendship. Or maybe you grow. Maybe you lose an employee. Or maybe you build a culture. Maybe you lose the battle. Or maybe you win the war. Fight anyway, not just for yourself, but for something bigger than you.

When David decided to rush to the battle line to defeat his enemy, that victory was for the entire nation. When I ran to the battle line to fight against racism and injustice, that fight was for the countless black people who feel like they don't have a voice. It was for my white brothers and sisters who didn't know what to do. I ran to the battle line for everyone who was looking for answers to questions they were afraid to ask. I didn't run from the battle, I ran to it.

After David defeated Goliath, he took Goliath's sword and cut the giant's head off, signifying his defeat. (I told you there were no referees). The battle was won and the people were saved. David would go on to win many more battles soon after. But it wasn't until he learned a valuable lesson: to run to the battle line.

What lies are you believing about yourself? Where are you running away from the battle instead of running toward it? Whose armor are you wearing? These questions will need to be answered within yourself before you can win against anyone else.

Be Illogical:

**Take charge.** In order to win the war between faith and fear, you must let faith be the aggressor.

**Don't let someone else's fear become your own.** When you're illogical, others will be scared enough for the both of you—that's fine, they can watch you take charge and overcome.

**Fight the way that fits you.** Drop the helmet of bronze and pick up your smooth stones.

**Others benefit from your victory.** When you win your own personal war within, the people around you, cities, and maybe even nations will also reap the benefits.

Don't let other people's
fears become your own.

     #illogicalbook

# 7

---

# Pick It Up

My time in the NFL was full of highs and lows, ups and downs. I had been cut five times by the age of twenty-five and traded after my rookie season. And though I started a few games over the course of my career, my success didn't come without a cost. Fear, doubt, and confusion ensued. Especially in the days leading up to the darkest day in football: cut day.

Cut day in the NFL is the first Monday in September. It's when the roster drops from ninety players to fifty-three; ancillary to essential. Nearly a thousand aspiring football players' dreams die that day. Over thirty per team. Each career coming to a screeching halt. The news is delivered in one of two ways. If you happen to be in the building, you'll receive a tap on the shoulder from someone affectionately known as the grim reaper. In the locker room, the grim reaper isn't some fictional character with a black hood and a scythe. No, the grim reaper is your GM (general manager) and more often than not they're going to tell you about the death of your NFL career, or at least with that team. He'll tap you and tell you a simple phrase, "Coach needs to see you, bring your playbook." No one in football wants that tap and many players choose not to go into the building that day. In that case, the reaper calls you.

Have you ever expected bad news? You knew it was coming but tried to do everything in your power to avoid it. You screened calls, dodged places you usually frequent, even slept in later than usual, hoping that the nightmare of your expectations would decide not to come true. You know what you're evading and the reaper does too. That's why when he calls, it's always without identification.

I learned not to pick up. During my playing days, whenever that extremely unwelcome unknown caller ID number showed up on my phone, I already knew who it was and what it was about. I was being released. Each ring felt like a vibration in my soul, each tremble a not-so-subtle reminder that my dreams of making an NFL team could be deferred once again. I hated that time of year. On one occasion, I made the team on Monday only to have my phone ring on Tuesday afternoon. No caller ID. The team had found a different player to fill a more pressing need. The reaper was calling to let me know. I was shaken.

Five days after the first episode of *Uncomfortable Conversations with a Black Man* was released, I was downing a bowl of Cheerios while scrolling through Twitter in my Austin townhouse. It was a Saturday around 8:00 a.m. and I was trying to figure out what I would do for the second episode. If I can be honest with y'all, I was hesitant to do another because of the success of the first one. That video was at about

25 million views and I didn't want to follow it up with something lesser.

As I sat there, cold spoon in hand, finishing off my cereal, my phone rang. It was a no-caller-ID number. I hadn't played in the NFL for years at this point, but I couldn't help flashing back to cut days and those dreaded calls from the reaper. Everything in me didn't want to answer that call even though I knew there were no teams needing my playbook back. Something told me that despite all the tension in my body, I needed to answer that phone call. So, I picked up.

"Acho," the voice began. "McConaughey speaking. I saw your first episode of *Uncomfortable Conversations with a Black Man*. I want to have a conversation."

I'm sitting there thinking to myself, "McConaughey? Liiiiike, Matthew McConaughey?" But don't worry, I played it cool and told him I would be recording episode two in four days.

"Tomorrow ... let's do it tomorrow!" he said. Now when an Academy Award winner cold-calls you and says he wants to share the camera with you to help fight for good in the world, you make it work. So, I did.

We spent an hour or so on the phone talking

through ideas and the next day, I sat down with Matthew McConaughey for the second episode of *Uncomfortable Conversations with a Black Man*.

Seventy-two hours after the release of episode two, I got a call from Oprah, also with unknown caller ID, of course. She had seen my show and wanted to help me on my journey. From there, the calls wouldn't stop coming. And this time, I was prepared to face what was on the other end.

Imagine if I never answered those calls? A pattern had happened in my earlier career: unidentified phone calls meant failure. This was so solidified in my mind that even years later, I almost didn't pick up Matthew McConaughey's call. I almost didn't pick up because of the fear of the way it had always been, but as we've discussed, you can only dream when you look to break out of the pattern. One call led to another call led to another call, and soon I had reframed my entire view on that buzzing screen with the word "Unknown" blasted across the top.

So many of us are keeping our lives from moving forward because of the patterns we've experienced before, because logically these patterns continue. **We need to always keep ourselves open to the possibility that this time it will be different. This is your chance.** This moment is the moment you've been waiting for. With belief in yourself and your truth, there might just be something better, greater, on the other end. Letting ourselves fall into the trap of expecting the worst generates the worst. But when we are open to our expectations being completely blown away, we open ourselves up to our dreams and the possibility of changing our communities and ourselves for the better.

Be Illogical:

**Forget past patterns.** The whole point of following your dreams is to shake up the mundane life that hasn't been feeding you! Forget the way things have always been and believe that they can change.

**Pick up the phone.** By this I mean always be open to there being greatness on the other side of something scary. Yes, for me an unknown phone call used to mean failure, but imagine if I had let that keep me from answering the call that led to one of the greatest conversations of my life and many other moments.

**Embrace the unknown.** At times it may literally be an unknown caller, but I mean this in every sense. Lean into uncertainty. Lean into things you don't already have the answers for. Don't get lost in predictions and patterns, just believe in what you are doing and move forward.

We need to always keep ourselves open to the possibility that **THIS TIME IT WILL BE DIFFERENT.** This is your chance.

# 8

---

# The First Drop of Rain

You may know of a man named Noah who built an ark. As the story goes, the world was evil then—people had been murdering one another and God wasn't happy. He wanted to start over, start anew. And he knew just the way to do it. God was going to send a flood over all the earth. Water would come from both the ground and the sky. Rain had never fallen before. At that time, the concept of a flood was literally incomprehensible.

Everything and everyone would be swept away unless you were on a special boat. Noah was tasked by God to build this boat (an "ark," to be technical) and bring on board a pair of every animal and a select few people. The boat was to be 145 meters long, 24 meters wide, and 14½ meters tall. That is massive. To provide some context, the *Titanic* was 269 meters long, roughly 1.8 times the length of Noah's project. And Noah did it all by himself. It took him over fifty years.

Minute by minute, hour by hour, month by month, year by year, he kept on building so that he would be ready for something no one had ever seen before. Imagine the ridicule he must have received from those closest to him. Before he could explain to his wife and kids why he was building a boat, he had to explain to them what rain even was. Historians and theologians debate whether the earth had ever seen rain as biblical texts lead you to believe it hadn't. Imagine the comments from the community, the flak. People walking by him on the way to the market asking, "Hey, Noah, you still waiting on that rain?" But he kept building. His continued to hammer in nail after nail even though the sky was clear and each passing day was sunnier than the one before.

Then it happened: God told Noah to board the boat. Noah lined up the animals two by two and boarded with his family. I imagine it like this: Noah is sitting inside the finished ark with countless splinters in his hand. He hears the rumble. He isn't sure what it is so he curiously peeks his head out a window. He looks left, right, left again, and then he feels it. Something smacks him between his brows. He blinks, then slowly raises his hand to his face as the first-ever drop of rain rolls down his forehead toward the bridge of his nose. "It can't be," he thinks. It was.

The rain signaled the demise of all those who didn't believe—who didn't heed the warning and board the boat. I imagine them pounding on the hull, begging Noah to let them on. But it was too late. The doors were shut and the waters started to rise. The moment Noah had been waiting for was finally here. He was ready for this.

Readers, your first drop of rain is coming and when it does, be ready because after that comes the flood. The flood of belief, the flood of blessings, the flood that will carry you to living out your destiny. You just have to believe and build. Build when you get the splinter in your hand, build when you get ridiculed by friends. Build out your dreams, your future. Keep a keen ear to the sky; the thunder is coming and with it, the rain.

Oprah Gail Winfrey was a news anchor in Nashville in the early 1970s. The youngest and first black female anchor at her local station, she soon transitioned to the bigger market in Baltimore and then to Chicago, which she would call home for the next forty years. In the television industry, the first drop of rain had hit Oprah, but boy, was there a flood to come.

By 1986, Oprah had taken the lowest-rated talk show in Chicago and made it the highest-rated. She then expanded the show from thirty minutes to one hour and renamed it *The Oprah Winfrey Show*. Shortly thereafter, her show's audience was double that of the number-one talk show in America, at that time led by Phil Donahue.

By 1988, Oprah was on top of an industry completely dominated and led by white men. In February 1993 she sat down with Michael Jackson for a primetime interview. Watched by over 36 million people, it is the most-watched interview in television history. The next year, Oprah was inducted into the National Women's Hall of Fame. For the next twenty-five years, she dominated the talk show space until she decided to step away from her daily show in 2011.

So, what can we learn from Oprah? (Well, besides everything.) There's an illogical lesson if you pay close enough attention to the details. Her raindrop hit in the '70s, when she was the youngest female news anchor at her local station. It was sufficiently pouring by the '80s, when she was given her own show. She was ready to handle the flood.

After your first drop of rain, there comes a moment when you have a decision to make. You either relax and say to yourself, "I did it!" or you welcome the flood with open arms. Oprah's mission toward greatness wasn't quenched after she became the anchor of local news, nor after she became host of *The Oprah Winfrey Show*. Her desire to impact the world was just beginning. She believed she could change an industry not through salacious scandals, but through compassionate conversation. She put on her earmuffs and paid no mind to the critics who refused to believe that a woman—let alone a black woman—could dominate an industry led by men. She experienced her first drop of rain when her Chicago show was renamed after her and that is when she truly began to shift the world. It was no longer a flood, it was her flood, and she had built a boat to carry her toward her dream.

You'll never be ready to handle the rain unless you start building your boat. Start singing, writing, dancing, listening, learning. Whatever your boat is—your dreams, your ideas, your passions, your hopes—start building.

What boats do you want to build? The rain is coming, it always does. Will you be ready?

Be Illogical:

**The flood is coming.** Perseverance is key. You just have to be hopeful, remain faithful, build, and wait for your first drop of rain.

**Don't let the rain catch you by surprise.** If Noah had been slacking, waking up every day and just chilling with his friends from the neighborhood instead of working, when it was time for the flood, he wouldn't have been ready. Don't let your opportunity catch you by surprise.

**Don't let everyone on your boat.** When your success is imminent, after people see the first drop of rain in your life, you better believe they're going to try to get on your boat. You can't let everyone on, otherwise you'll sink.

You'll never be ready to handle the rain unless you **START BUILDING YOUR BOAT.**

# 9

---

# Let the Games Begin

During the 2016 season, Steph Curry, the slender-built twenty-seven-year-old point guard from Charlotte, North Carolina, led the Golden State Warriors to an NBA-record-setting seventy-three wins. It was the greatest regular-season record by any team in the history of the NBA. As a result of his team's success and his own mind-boggling individual accolades, Curry was the first-ever person to be named the league's MVP unanimously. But before the flood of success came for him in 2016, there was a drop of rain in 2015 . . . well, several drops actually.

You see, in 2015 Curry also won the MVP award en route to winning the Warriors' first championship in forty years. Curry also broke the record for three-point field goals made in a season with 286, and seemingly out of nowhere became the face of the NBA. So between the 2015 and 2016 seasons, he went from being the hunter to the hunted. But for Curry, that's when the games truly began. The next year, the Warriors, the reigning NBA champions, again finished in first place in the Western Conference, but their sixty-seven regular-season wins from the prior year weren't enough. They won an NBA record seventy-three games in 2016 (out of eighty-two). Curry crushed his own NBA record of three-point field goals made with a whopping 402 during that season, a record we may not see broken in our lifetime. Say what you will about Jordan, LeBron, and Kobe, but even they never accomplished the feats Curry did that season.

The NBA three-point line ranges from twenty-two feet to twenty-three feet and nine inches.

Curry shoots from way beyond that mark. And crazy enough, he shoots better the farther away he is. During the 2015–2016 season, Curry made 51.6 percent of his shots between twenty-eight feet and half court. He made 46.1 percent of his shots from the three-point line that season. The more illogical the shot, the more likely he was to make it. Why? Because Steph wasn't afraid to try. "I might be delusional," he said in an interview, "but I feel like I can get better at putting the ball in the basket." He made that statement in 2018, and, well, it's 2022 and Curry is still shooting at an enormously proficient rate. He's become more and more accurate and more and more illogical as the years have gone on. He will go down as the best shooter in the history of basketball and he's still getting better. If you don't believe me, just go watch an NBA game. Look for the guy draining threes from half court.

Speaking of world-class athletes pushing limits, Usain Bolt attended the 2016 Olympics as his last, but they would absolutely be the most memorable. He had won gold in two consecutive one-hundred-meter dashes, the first athlete to ever accomplish that feat. But this race would prove to be the most challenging. Why? Because halfway through he was in fourth place. Usain Bolt is an eight-time Olympic gold medalist. The race that made him most famous was the one-hundred-meter dash, a race in which he holds the world record of 9.58 seconds. Less than the ten-second timer on *Wheel of Fortune*. Bolt had experienced myriad successes. He had won the event in the 2008 Olympics in Beijing, then followed up that performance with another first-place finish in London in 2012. Even though I played professional football, track is my first love. There's nothing more exhilarating to me than watching two people at the height of their athletic ability competing for one prize: a gold medal. You can imagine how excited I was when I got to watch Bolt try to defend his crown some eight years after initially winning it. After being at the very top of his game. At the top of his field. I was ready to see greatness. I was ready to see the number-one sprinter in history blow everyone away. I was ready for dominance, but what I got was something completely different. The world champion, the greatest sprinter of all time, was in fourth place.

I always wondered what that would be like. To be the best, to be fastest, but to be behind. Would you lose your technique? Would you abandon your form? Or would you be illogical? Bolt chose the latter. "When I go on that track," he began, "it's like I transform. The confidence I have when I'm out there is different. No matter how far you think you are ahead of me I'm going to catch you."* He was right. Bolt had been running track since he was a kid. He had been striking his famous lightning bolt pose since he was a young boy running the streets of Jamaica. He knew he had the skill, and even though things didn't look great, he trusted his technique, reached for the illogical, and won the race. It was his third straight gold in the one-hundred-meter dash. He was the first ever to accomplish this feat.

No one else in history had ever done what Usain Bolt did *before* those 2016 games. He was the fastest, but he got faster. He sped up. He stepped on the gas. In doing so, he reminded us all of the most illogical truth yet. When you're on your path to being illogical and you make a little headway, the only way to go is faster.

Ditching logic and opening ourselves up to striving for the impossible or for more than what someone else might deem good enough leads to

---

* https://www.youtube.com/watch?v=SYK1Osn-dys

the limitless life you've been holding yourself back from.

After the first episode of *Uncomfortable Conversations with a Black Man* went viral, I almost pivoted. I almost let that unforeseen success deter me from what I knew to be best—that it was time to step on the gas. The next two episodes were just the beginning. After I recorded with Matthew McConaughey, Chip and Joanna Gaines reached out and asked if their family could join. Following the impact that episode had, I decided to have a conversation with a mixed-race family who also lived in Texas. White parents with white, black, and mixed kids. The games had begun.

I produced every episode and procured each guest. Everything I needed to be successful was already in place. That's the thing about being illogical: when it first starts to drizzle, don't change anything you've been doing. Use all of your experiences and resources to take you even further.

After I met with Oprah, she asked about my future aspirations with the series. I told her that I wanted to make *Uncomfortable Conversations* into a book. Her response caught me off guard. "Books?!" she said, her ears perking up. "I love books. Can you get it done in two months?" I said yes. For context, many books take years to write. I had eight weeks. Oprah and the team knew that the need for a book like this, tackling racism with conversation, was too great, and they wanted to publish it that November. I had work to do. The games were now in full swing. I had a full-time job along with other interviews and conversations to record, but I still found time to write. And with a lot of help from the team around me, we got it done. That book, my first book, became a *New York Times* bestseller.

Writing *Uncomfortable Conversations with a Black Man* proved to be one of the most important projects I've ever worked on. Videos can go viral but written words last forever. I needed to maximize the moment and put something on paper that would affect the masses. I wanted to create something that could be passed down from generation to generation. Something that would have lasting impact.

I was recently having a conversation with a friend of mine. He again brought up the idea of a children's book. "Kids books," he said, "are inevitably read to them by their parents. Imagine the impact you could make on families if you created something for young adults in addition to what you created for parents."

I did. I adapted my book into an edition for young readers. I poured my heart out into that book, thinking about my experiences growing up as a minority in a majority culture. I wanted to save kids from some of the headache and heartache that I had faced as a black boy growing up in America. Thus *Uncomfortable Conversations with a Black Boy* was born. A book that would reach a younger, more impressionable audience. A book that could change generations. Then seven days after publication, I got a call from my book agent.

"I hope it's good news," I said, knowing that the one-week mark is when you find out where your book ranks on the bestsellers list.

"Emmanuel, you may want to sit down for this."

I didn't. *Uncomfortable Conversations with a Black Man* had debuted at number three. Now, for *Uncomfortable Conversations with a Black Boy*, nothing less than number one would do. I had been living an illogical life, believing an impossible belief, and I wasn't ready for that belief to be a lie. I had won a few races, but I refused to slow down. I wanted gold. I had also been living with the pain of people's doubts for so long. The chants, the loneliness, the empty fields. I wanted some kind of validation to show that I was on the right course. It's illogical to believe that you could make a video about injustice that would get millions of views and become a bestselling author in the span of a few short months. All while doing something that you believed was and still is your service to the world. I had to go harder.

And then she spoke. "We got number one! We're number-one *New York Times* bestsellers! Emmanuel, YOU are a number-one *New York Times* bestselling author."

I smiled. My brother was with me in LA when I heard the news. Before he could say anything, I looked at him, nodded my head, and winked. You see, I had learned that the worst thing you can do when the game is in play is to get up from the table and walk away. You have to believe even when no one else will. Book agents, family, and friends all told me that you couldn't write a book in two months. That I'd be hard-pressed to be a bestseller, let alone a number-one *New York Times* bestseller. They said that the market was oversaturated. That a book like this is too narrow, that it wouldn't sell. But no one else has to be right, only you.

I had pushed beyond the boundaries and worked hard. I was due for a vacation, and I had the perfect one planned: four days out of the country with three close friends. And then my phone rang. There was some controversy surrounding *The Bachelor*, the most-watched unscripted show on national TV. I was asked to fill in as the host for the legendary "After the Final Rose" episode.

"Some controversy" is an understatement. Pictures had surfaced of Rachael Kirkconnell, the winning contestant, at an Old South antebellum-themed party just a few years prior. It was a bad look, but the response from Chris Harrison, the host of *The Bachelor*, was received even more poorly. He used phrases like "woke police" and insinuated that it was okay for Rachael to attend the party because everyone else did. Comments like those are, in many ways, the reason that the *Uncomfortable Conversations with a Black Man* videos and book were so necessary. For people to learn how to communicate better and love better.

I was smack dab in the middle of my vacation but when the phone rang with this opportunity, I decided to cut my vacation short in order to record. Opportunities like this only come once in a lifetime, and when you get them, you have to take advantage. You have to step on the gas.

Recording the "After the Final Rose" episode was the single most difficult thing I've ever done on television. I had been having difficult discussions about race for months, and now I had to have one on a national stage in front of an enormous audience. I was tasked with navigating a conversation around love, race, and the outcome of three different relationships in front of a dedicated viewership. Remember, your calling will call you, you just have to pick up—even if it means cutting your vacation a few days short.

If you want to be illogical, take everything we've talked about doing up to this point and do it more. Do it better. **Once you go against logic, don't be surprised when it works**. Keep going. Step on the gas. You may already be living illogically. If you are, the only way to go is up. Just ask Steph Curry or Usain Bolt.

Be Illogical:

**Step on the gas.** A good start is undermined if you tail off at the fifty-meter mark, and you can't win the race with a strong finish if you are too far out of it. Similarly, when you begin to make headway, and are just a few moments away from achieving greatness, that's when you must step on the gas.

**Stay focused.** Usain Bolt's dominance was challenged during the 2016 Olympic Games. Forty meters into the race, he was astonishingly in fourth place. Bolt maintained his focus and ultimately caught every single individual ahead of him, going on to win the race and, in his usual fashion, he struck a lightning bolt pose moments after crossing the finish line. When you stop logic from limiting your potential, you may find yourself behind during the course of your race. That's fine—just stay focused, keep running, and prepare to strike your pose at the end of the race.

**Don't let the pressure get to you.** The higher you climb up a mountain the harder it is to breathe, because the air is thinner at high altitude. But that doesn't tell the whole story. The reason it is so difficult to breathe at high altitudes is because the pressure from within you, your lungs, is greater than the pressure outside of you, the air. As the impossible in your life becomes more probable, and your dreams begin to manifest, don't let the pressure from within get to you.

Once you go against logic,
# DON'T BE SURPRISED
# WHEN IT WORKS.

  #illogicalbook

# 10

---

# When the Dam Breaks

Show me who makes a profit from war, and I'll show you how to stop that war.

—HENRY FORD

In 1968, children were dying, people were starving, and my father was fighting. The Nigerian Civil War, also known as the Biafran War, had just begun the year before. Southeastern Nigeria, or Biafra, wanted freedom from its northern counterpart. Fundamental differences in leadership, ideology, and government, along with unfair British policies and a severe distrust after independence from British colonization, caused a rift that was too large to repair.

Kids as young as sixteen would fight in this war. My father, Onyebuchi Sunday Acho, or "Sonny," was one of them. He wasn't supposed to fight but his dad had died, he was the oldest son, and his family had no food to eat. So, he ran to the battle line and volunteered himself even though he was under the proper age. He was accepted.

The Biafran War took the lives of approximately three million Nigerians. A majority of them were Igbos, one of the main tribes of the Nigerian people. My dad is Igbo. In addition to the war, two thousand children died every single day from a disease known as kwashiorkor, a form of malnutrition from a lack of protein. It killed an estimated two million people, half of them children. Food supplies were cut off by land, sea, and air. The losses became too much to bear. Biafra surrendered, but not until the damage was done.

It was known as the world's first televised war. People from all around saw the damage that was being done, the children who were being starved.

People like John Lennon and Martin Luther King Jr. protested. My dad would survive, but not without his fair share of casualties. One of his bunkmates was killed in a blast. He saw it firsthand and still has wounds from the shrapnel. It makes very little sense that he's still here today.

When the war ended, my father wanted a better life not only for him but for his lineage as well. He realized that if he was going to impact the world, it would be hard to do so from a desolate, poverty-stricken country. He was determined to break through and change his life and those of his loved ones, to break the dam for the generations to come. He just wasn't sure how yet.

At one point in time, scientists believed it was impossible to run a mile in under four minutes as they didn't believe that the human body was physically capable of such a feat. But if it were ever to be done, it would have to be in the most pristine of conditions: 68 degrees with no wind. Scientists subscribed to that logic, the general population subscribed to that logic, even professional runners subscribed to that logic. But not Roger Bannister.

It was a cold and windy day on a wet track. Bannister

hadn't meant to go for the record that day. He was going to save his strength for a different meet ten days later; he was going to submit to the science. But while at the starting line, the wind died down and Bannister made his decision. He was going to go for the record. He was going to break the dam.

The race began and Bannister was off. He finished the first two of the four laps in a time of 1 minute and 58 seconds. Lap three would prove to be a struggle, but he completed it at 3:00.7. One more lap to go. If Bannister was going to go for this record, he needed a final push. One that he had mastered while training alone for years. No fancy gyms like Orange Theory or Equinox, no personal trainer. Just him, his earmuffs, and his childlike faith. He didn't have much, but he had his belief, his skill, and his will. His will to disregard logic and do the unthinkable.

The fourth lap ended and the emcee began to announce the time. The crowd in the stands waited eagerly, wondering if they had just witnessed history. They had: 3 minutes and 59.4 seconds. Bannister had done the impossible; the dam had been broken. The world would never be the same. Because scientists, the "experts," believed it couldn't be done, all runners did as well. Their actions followed their belief. The dam that needed to be broken—that was broken that day—isn't physical, it's mental.

Forty-six days after Bannister made the record, an Australian by the name of John Landy went on to break the four-minute mile as well, with a time of three minutes and fifty-eight seconds. And within the next two years, ten other runners did what no one had done in nearly two thousand years. This wasn't because of an advancement in technology or new training techniques, but simply because one man decided to disregard limits, cast aside logic, and break the dam. Bannister did the unthinkable and the running world hasn't been the same since. Over the last sixty years, the world record in the mile has dropped another seventeen seconds and now high school kids are running miles in under four minutes. What was once deemed "scientifically impossible" now happens more often than anyone would have imagined. The four-minute-mile barrier is still celebrated by distance runners whenever they achieve it, but that celebration started with one individual. Roger Bannister "might have been crazy" to attempt what he did, but now, as we all can see, he was perfectly sane. And he was masterfully illogical.

When you are illogical, cracks begin to form in the dam. The games have just begun, so keep running and break the dam. Go for the unthinkable. When you do, you'll change not only your life, but also the lives of those around you, breaking the dam and letting others follow through.

It may not seem like breaking out of generations of war and struggle and running less than a four-minute mile are the same, but each man defied the odds, however different those odds may have been. My dad was determined to break his own dam. After a new currency was put in place during the war, the Biafran currency was deemed unusable. Each Biafran was given twenty Nigerian pounds regardless of the amount of wealth they had had beforehand, and their only hope was to find ways to build wealth and create a new life. My dad became a local preacher, preaching and teaching on buses. No, not on moving buses, on the broken-down, stationary kind that are no longer good for transit. He found joy in doing this, but unfortunately for him, his family wasn't too thrilled.

Preaching on top of buses was not one of the ways you could build wealth or create a new life. But my dad felt as though it was his calling. His mother questioned him and his brothers laughed at him, but my father refused to listen. He put his earmuffs on and spoke like his life depended on it. Because it did.

A few months later, some American missionaries came to town offering physical and spiritual assistance. They came to preach to people like my dad . . . and then they met my dad. At first, all they heard was a voice full of passion, energy, excitement, and vigor. But the crowd was too big. That's when my dad took a higher position. He's not the tallest individual, so he climbed on top of a nearby bus. When he spoke again, everybody listened, including the missionaries. After spending a week with him, they were left utterly impressed and asked if he would be willing to come to America to share his passion with those who needed a spark. My dad was faced with the opportunity of a lifetime. A chance to change the trajectory of the lives of generations to come. He had run to the battle line in war to change his family's circumstance and he would run to a different battle line now. He obliged and just like that, he said goodbye to his family and boarded a plane to America for the first time ever, not knowing what was on the other side.

When my dad first came to America, he had no idea what to expect. He had been living in a country where people were drinking water from plastic bags and eating whatever they could to get by. As you drove through the streets of Lagos, those trying to make ends meet would slap the glass of passenger windows as they held bags of water in their other hand. On the driver's side, you'd see an individual shoving strung-up rats over the glass and into your face. The rats were dead—the objective wasn't to scare you but to convince you to buy the rat poison they were selling. These were the circumstances. This was life.

No one in my father's family had ever left the country, let alone the continent. Yet here he was, in America. Over the next several years, he would travel back and forth to teach, preach, and eventually continue his education. He would bring his wife with him and start a new family in a new country. They would work as a janitors and at fast food restaurants while pursuing their master's and, ultimately, doctoral degrees.

My father left home to find home. He put down roots, built community, and became a beacon of hope for everyone in his homeland. The dam had been broken and a door had been opened for my dad, his mother, his brothers, his sisters, and his village. Generations were changed. He would go on to have kids (shout-out to me) who would do their best to change their communities as well. All because he wasn't afraid and refused to let preconceived limits hold him back.

My father knew that there was more. There had to be. More than just taking a job to make ends meet, more than listening to other people's expectations for his life, more than living logically. That singular decision to go against logic and follow his dream before he knew anything would come of it paid off big. Many believed that him going to live in America was impossible at worst, illogical at best. America was simply a country you see in movies; it was not actually a place that could ever be called home. In the late 1970s, roughly a decade removed from the Biafran War, a trip from the villages of Nigeria to America was about as realistic as a trip to Narnia. But my father refused to be limited by what other people believed. He wasn't afraid of someone else's fear. He would be the agent of change that an entire community would benefit from.

My father is from a small village in Nigeria. One of seven children, he lost his father and sister and fought in a war all before the age of eighteen. Yet somehow, he found himself using his life as a gift for others. He dreamed of a better life for him and his family, his community, anyone under his circle of influence. He dreamed he could break the dam, and he did.

Once the structure of a dam has been torn down, whether mental or physical, it is near impossible to put a stop to the water that is now freely flowing. And that's a good thing. Broken dams, specifically those of the mind, show people that the impossible is only impossible until you do it. Just like my dad surviving a war that killed over two million people and following his passion rather than living in fear. The fact that he's alive gives me hope. I hope that it gives you hope too. Take the limits off of your mind. Hop on that flight and go to the other side.

Now, the majority of my father's immediate and extended family members have made lives in America, Europe, and all around the world. Both his sons (my brother and I) enjoyed NFL careers and currently work on television. One daughter has a doctorate degree while the other works in the prenatal intensive care unit as a nurse practitioner. My father broke the dam. His belief allowed others like me to believe as well, and his success was not only his, but benefited generations to come. Yours will too.

Yes, they both broke different dams, but it turns out that my father and Bannister had another thing in common. Roger Bannister would run a few more times before he retired and went into medicine. I always found that interesting. Why would someone who just accomplished a seemingly impossible feat choose to walk away from his fame? It didn't make sense to me. But then I did some research. Bannister had been affected by war himself. As a boy, he'd heard air-raid sirens during the Battle of Britain in World War II. When he heard the sirens, like those children in the villages in Nigeria hearing gunshots, he would often run for safety.

Bannister tapped into that experience as a professional athlete. In his memoir he writes, "I imagined bombs and machine guns raining on me if I didn't go my fastest. Was this a little of the feeling I have now before I shoot into the lead and am afraid of a challenge down the finishing straight? To move into the lead means making an attack requiring fierceness and confidence, but fear must play some part in the last stage when no relaxation is possible and all discretion is thrown to the winds." Fierceness and confidence. All discretion thrown to the winds. That is what I'm asking of you, no matter what race you are running. I believe that Bannister and Dr. Acho are asking the same. Throw fear, discretion, and logic to the winds and race with ferocity and confidence into the record books.

When my dad boarded that plane to America, I doubt he knew what dams he was breaking for his family, for his community. New lives have been created. New destinies have been fulfilled. When Bannister broke the four-minute-mile barrier, he broke a dam for every runner to come and change the limits of running as we knew them. The fact that you are alive today is reason to celebrate. Your life alone could very well break the dam that someone needs to see. **Don't give up and don't wait for anyone else to do what you are destined for.**

Be Illogical:

**Be the first to imagine the unimaginable.** It's only impossible until you do it. Remember within the very word you find "I'm possible."

**Breaking the dam lets others through.** My dad broke the dam and as a result my life changed, and hopefully I have the ability to also change lives. Don't just do it for you.

**When the dam is broken, it is broken forever.** The saying "Seeing is believing" is because our eyes rule our actions. Once you have finally accomplished something once believed to be impossible, doing it again is no longer difficult.

# DON'T GIVE UP
and don't wait for
anyone else to do what
you are destined for.

 #illogicalbook

# 11

## Goals Are Dumb

had two goals my senior year in high school: to win homecoming king and to win Athlete of the Year. In my sophomore year, I had committed to play football at the University of Texas. My grades were good as well. So by my senior year, the only thing left was to garner these two accolades—and nothing was going to get in my way, or so I thought. I attended St.

Mark's School of Texas, a small college preparatory school in Dallas. It was an all-boys school where we wore a mandated uniform. Gray slacks and a white button-down. I was in school among geniuses and national merit scholars. True story, a kid in the grade above me won the national spelling bee, the one you see on TV. "Pococurante" was his winning word. Anyway, you get the point. My school was full of brilliant minds, but I had carved out a nice spot for myself as the reasonably smart "jock." We had seventy-five people in my graduating class and I was the only one going to college on a full athletic scholarship. I had led our team to the state championship in football, led the team in scoring in basketball, and had set school records in track and field. I was well-known, well-liked, and well-respected. Then, when homecoming nominations came around, I found out that I wasn't even nominated. I was baffled. And yes, I'm still upset. After a little bit of digging, I found out the reason my name was left off the ballot. Someone said that since my brother had won it the year before, the school didn't want to risk me winning it this year. They didn't want to create an "Acho dynasty." So they left me off the ballot to ensure I wouldn't win. I was discouraged but not dismayed, yet. I still had a chance to win Athlete of the Year at the end of the school banquet, and no bias was going to stop that.

Spencer Gym was quiet. The auditorium had been transformed from a basketball gym to a banquet hall. Tables were set, lights were lit, the night had begun. My entire family showed up to the event. They knew how important this award was to me, so they traveled near and far to celebrate what was sure to be my big night. We had a table near the front and my parents couldn't have been prouder. Even my two older sisters, who were both in college at the time, had come to this event. It was the penultimate event before graduation and my last family weekend before I went off to college. We were dressed to the nines. All of us eagerly awaiting the moment that my name would be called. The presenter began, "The winner for Athlete of the Year is . . . Ben Grisz."

"Excuse me, you misspelled and misspoke my name," I thought. Athlete of the Year, my only remaining goal for my high school career, and someone else was chosen. I was shocked, I was embarrassed, I was ashamed. Everyone had shown up to celebrate me, and now, there was nothing to celebrate. Anyone who knows me knows that I'm not much of a crier. I always try to find the silver lining to keep me joyful. There was no silver lining. The lining was black, pitch black. As a matter of fact, there was no lining at all. I bawled my eyes out, I wept uncontrollably. Something about this loss was different. This time, it felt like the award had been taken from me. Stripped from my gripping hands. While crying real and heavy tears that night, I learned a life-altering lesson: **The easiest way to fail in life is to set a goal**.

While I learned that lesson in high school, I was late in applying it to my life. By the conclusion of my junior year in college, I submitted a proposal to the NFL to assess my draft value. My goal was always to graduate a year early, leave school with my brother, and be selected in the NFL draft before him (ha!). Rounds one, two, or three were the goal. Sam and I played together in college, and though I was a year younger, I was ready. I'd done the work to prepare. I liked my odds. Then I got back the report. It read as follows: "Emmanuel Acho Draft Projection: ROUNDS LATE ROUND-UNDRAFTED." In layman's terms, the talent evaluators projected I was not good enough to be selected early in that year's NFL draft, if I were to be selected at all.

I was again devastated. Ever since I was a kid, I had the dream of getting drafted in the NFL. And now I was being told I would be a late-round draft or undrafted. It didn't make any sense to me. I had been fixated on this goal since I was a child and now the possibility of that future reality was being taken away. I decided to return to college for my senior year and go after my goal once again: to be selected in the first three rounds of the NFL draft, higher than my brother—I can't help it, I'm competitive. Then I saw a Harvard Business School study on goal setting stating that the 3 percent of Harvard MBA students who had clear written goals earned, on average, ten times as much as the other 97 percent. As you have likely learned, I'm very ambitious, so I took the projection letter, highlighted the words "Emmanuel Acho" and "LATE ROUND-UNDRAFTED," and taped the page above the headboard in my bedroom. I would read it every night before I went to sleep and every morning before I got out of bed. It was the first thing I saw when I opened my eyes and the last thing I saw before I closed them. That day I made up my mind that I would be a top-round pick in the next year's draft. A few months later, my brother was drafted in the early fourth round, pick 104 to be exact. My goal was still in place but now even more specific. Be pick 103. I'm sure some of you can relate to a little sibling rivalry.

I did everything in my power to increase my draft stock. I set records for the school, changed my physique, and became even more mentally sharp on and off the field. There were no deterrents, no distractions. I knew my draft stock would rise. It had to with all the work I was putting in. By season's end, my draft projection did indeed rise. What was initially a fourth- to seventh-round or undrafted projection after my junior year had now risen to a second- to fifth-round projection after my senior year. I could see the dedication paying off. All that was left was to make it through the pre-draft process while staying healthy. I had to attend a few private team workouts here and there, and the invite-only NFL Combine, where you run a few sprints and lift weights in front of the coaches. If I did these final few things well, I was sure to reach the goal I had set out to accomplish years before. The goal I spent days thinking about and nights dreaming about, the one I had written down, focused on, and aimed for. But then, a few weeks before the draft, I heard a pop.

I was performing a sprint drill at the NFL Combine in front of the head coaches and owners of all thirty-two NFL teams, when there was a pop heard round the world. The bang was so loud that I initially thought a gun had gone off. But then I realized the sound had come from me. The pop was my quad muscle tearing off the bone as I sprinted. I fell to the ground and screamed in pain. It was eight weeks before the draft, six months before the season, and I was sidelined. I had no idea what would happen now. Would I go in the top three rounds? Would I be drafted at all? I was crushed, but I was determined to make it back as soon as possible and see my dream come true. Of course I could still be drafted while injured, but the injury would drastically impact my draft status. In the NFL, the best ability is availability, and being injured means you're not available.

Two months went by of tireless training and rehab. It was now time to head to Dallas, where I would join family and friends to watch the draft together and see the fate of my NFL future. Round one came and my name wasn't called. I wasn't bothered; after all, my end goal was to go in the top three rounds, not exclusively round one. Rounds two and three took place the next day. This would be it. This would be the day I would reach my goal and live out my dream. But by the time the day was over I had heard nothing. Was it the injury? Was it a mistake? Was it my fault? These are questions I never learned the answers to, but what I did know, or at least what I felt, is that I failed. And after dreaming for so long and working so hard, it was impossible for me to come to terms with this failure.

I did end up getting drafted on day three, but it was no celebration. It was three rounds lower than I'd hoped, in the sixth round to the Cleveland Browns. Being drafted this late (there are only seven rounds of the current NFL draft) meant there was no guarantee of making an actual NFL roster. Rosters in the NFL are based on monetary commitment as much as they are on a player's talent level. The lower you get drafted, the less money you get paid. The less money you get paid, the less likely the team is to keep you around. I had given everything to reach this goal, yet I didn't get it. This failure did not just impact my net worth, but more important, my self-worth. I was at an all-time low.

Self-esteem is defined as "confidence in one's own worth or abilities." Self-efficacy is "an individual's confidence in their ability to achieve a task or complete a goal." Both my self-esteem and self-efficacy were dampened by my failures. And though I played for four years in the NFL, that experience scarred me. I lost a lot of self-confidence during that time and, quite frankly, that period probably aided in my decision to retire from the NFL so soon. Prior to that moment, I had accomplished nearly every goal I had put my mind to. But now something was different. Now it was time to stop setting goals.

Setting goals is the biggest misconception of achievement. Now, yes, there are obviously exceptions, and we'll get to those a little bit later, but our society conditions us to think of goal setting as the only way to get things done or get what we want. Goals are not the answer. Before you shut the book out of pure shock at that notion, let me explain. At best, a goal puts a ceiling on our achievement, often preventing us from dreaming of something greater or different. At worst, constant goal setting and failure to reach those goals threaten our self-efficacy and self-esteem. Let's say you set a goal and actually achieve it. Congratulations, you did it! But, what if you could've done more? The mind is incredibly powerful; when you set a goal, your brain will work toward that goal, but just that goal. We'll never know how fast Roger Bannister could've run if his goal was to run a mile in three minutes and fifty seconds instead of just under four minutes. Now let's say you set a goal for yourself but don't achieve it. You'll find yourself somewhat like me as a senior after losing Athlete of the Year. You may not have the heavy tears, but you'll surely be dejected, and begin to question your talent and ability in that area. If a goal becomes your singular focus in life, as it did with me, then not reaching that goal leads you to question your whole self and existence.

I feel so passionate about my aversion to goal setting that I committed my master's degree (in sports psychology) to studying goals. You cannot fully understand and explore the weaknesses of a subject unless you know the subject well. As I said before, there are, of course, some benefits to setting goals. One of the first reasons you set a goal is because it allows you to monitor any improvement you're making. By nature we're creatures seeking approval, we want to know how we fared on a task. That's partially why social media has such rampant success—we're obsessed with our performance, which social media catalogues meticulously in likes, follows, and engagement analytics. Did this picture garner more "likes" than our last? We long for a sense of feedback not only from others, but more important, from ourselves. This feedback is what goals provide. Goals allow you to track your progress, telling you when you've achieved a certain landmark, and also notifying you of shortcomings.

This need for feedback is further validated by being a prerequisite of the concept of flow. As defined in psychologist Mihaly Csikszentmihalyi's book *Flow: The Psychology of Optimal Experience*, flow is "a subjective state people report when they are completely involved in something to the point of forgetting time, fatigue, and everything else but the activity itself," and is widely considered the optimal state of being. Have you ever gotten lost in time while learning a new song on your favorite instrument, or maybe while painting a room of your house? Maybe even wasted hours away while trying to master the latest dance on TikTok? This is flow. Flow is difficult to achieve, but as Csikszentmihalyi notes in his book, its attainment is believed to be contingent upon a clear and defined set of goals.

There are other moments where I believe goals can add value. When the focal point changes from individual to communal or team settings, tangible goals are imperative. In the traditional working world, goals can be important, such as when deadlines may be crucial to collaborative projects. But in

our personal lives, we already have so many limitations put on us, why add more by setting limiting
goals that compromise our ability to make sweeping
impact?

So this begs the ultimate question: What is the
alternative to setting goals? The answer is simple,
**don't set a goal, have an objective with no lim-
itations**. The difference may seem minor, but this
small difference has major implications for your
achievement in life.

To most, the words "goal" and "objective" seem
interchangeable, but there is a small but very key
distinction. Merriam-Webster defines objective as
"something toward which effort is directed." There's
your distinction. An objective with no limitations
means seeking something without a defined ending.
A goal on the other hand is "the *end* toward which
effort is directed." Even the definition of the word
"goal" begins by talking about an ending. A goal is
finite, but when you set an objective without limitations, the possibilities are infinite. The word "goal"
you hear most frequently in the game of soccer. The
goal (pun intended) of the game is to score goals,
but you only ever hear that word pronounced when
one specific action takes place. For a minimum of
ninety game minutes, players sprint around a field

chasing after the ball. They devote all their time and energy to attaining possession of the object but they are only greeted with this ever-evasive word "goal" when one specific incident occurs—when the ball makes its way into the net. So if that is the goal, then what are all of the other actions? More important, if you never get the ball into your opponent's net over the course of the game, then what does that say about all the energy you expended? We've been indoctrinated with this belief that goals are great, but what if there's a better way?

When it comes to chasing your dreams, don't aim for one thing, direct your energy forward to an infinite number of outcomes. That way you don't miss. Aim to make as big of an impact in the world as possible. If you shoot at something, you just might hit something.

> But why aim for one thing when you can have **everything**?

In every decision I make now, I think about how much of an impact I can make on this world. When the opportunity arises, the impact follows. I don't miss. When it comes to choosing small, targeted goals versus huge, effective impact, always choose impact.

When I first got into media, people asked if I wanted to be the next Michael Strahan. My immediate response was always no. Michael Strahan achieved a lot. He transitioned masterfully from NFL star to media personality. I wasn't going to make that same mistake I had in pursuing the draft. No goals, nothing written down or plastered on a wall. I had one limitless objective: to be one of the most creative people the industry has ever seen. If I achieved the goal of being like Mike, the best I could ever be is like Mike. I could never reach my full potential. I could never be who I was meant to be. I could never create the things I was meant to create. No *Uncomfortable Conversations*, no creativity, no art. Now, some years later, I'm well on my way but I'm not thinking of the finish line.

Before moving on, I will concede to this. When an individual is responsible for their contributions to a team at large, goals may serve a purpose. When the focal point changes from individual to communal, goals can add value. In team settings, tangible goals are imperative. Take, for example, a relay team in track. Their goal is obviously to run fast, but elite speed is irrelevant without the proper exchanging of the baton. Without the baton traveling the full oval, all other individual race accomplishments are undermined. In the instance where there is a necessity for accountability from one athlete to another to fulfill their responsibility for the greater good of the team (properly exchanging the baton), a collective goal is necessary. In the traditional working world too, goals can be important, such as when deadlines may be crucial to collaborative projects. When a manager states to his or her employees that they have a deadline to meet by a specific date, meeting that deadline is the only factor of importance. Therefore, when group achievement is the focal point, and individuals are accountable to uphold their finite requirement, then goal setting is of value. But outside of specific instances such as these, don't set goals; create an objective with no limitations. Be illogical. Be free. Live a life without failure.

Be Illogical:

**Goals aren't everything.** We have been sold this dream that the only way to succeed is by setting goals, writing them down, and going for them. However, what I have found in my own life is that when you set a goal, you achieve that goal, but that goal only. Imagine how much more you can achieve if you do not limit yourself to a specific benchmark.

**Set yourself up for success.** Self-esteem and self-worth both start with the prefix "self," meaning they belong to you. Failed goals make you more susceptible to low amounts of self-esteem and self-worth.

**Don't live for the finish line.** Achieve flow not through aiming for one specific thing, but through living in the moment. Run your own race and see where it gets you. If you open up your peripheral vision to different paths, your impact is so much greater than crossing one finish line.

Don't set a goal;
# HAVE AN OBJECTIVE WITH
# NO LIMITATIONS.

  #illogicalbook

# 12

## Still Get Out of the Boat

Ruby Bridges was just six years old when she changed the course of history. She was born September 8, 1954, the same year the U.S. Supreme Court ruled to end racial segregation in schools. However, some Southern schools were slow to adopt this policy, as you might imagine. Ruby lived in Louisiana and at the age of five she was attending an all-black school. One year later the federal government stepped in and mandated public schools in Louisiana desegregate. The all-white school district that Ruby was located in created entrance exams for the black students in order to prevent some of them from attending. Despite this effort, Ruby and five other students got in. The Bridges family now had a decision to make. There was an all-white school merely a few blocks from the Bridges' family home: William Frantz Elementary. Ruby's dad did not want her to attend, but her mom insisted. She wanted Ruby to have the same education as her white counterparts so that she could have a chance at a better future. Her father conceded and Ruby was set to attend her all-white school. Three of the other five black students who passed the exam, nicknamed "the McDonough three," went to another all-white school: McDonough Elementary. The two other students could have accompanied Ruby at William Frantz Elementary, but they decided to stay at their all-black school. Ruby would have to do it alone.

On November 14, 1960, Ruby Bridges walked up to the doors of Frantz Elementary. She was met by a crowd of racist white individuals jeering her as she walked down the sidewalk toward the entrance, notebook in hand. She later recounted that the only time she was afraid was when she saw a white person in the crowd holding a black doll in a coffin. Imagine the courage, imagine the strength, imagine the fearlessness of this six-year-old girl who was willing to change history.

This moment in history brings to mind a story that is meaningful to me and that I hold close as I walk through life. Peter and his eleven friends were sitting on a boat in the middle of the sea when the winds and the waves began to beat against its sides. The waves didn't scare Peter—he and his brother were both fishermen by trade—but the ghost that then appeared on the water did.

Peter had witnessed miracles, as a follower of Jesus. He saw Jesus heal people and turn water into wine. I'm sure we all wish we had that ability. But now as the winds beat against the boat, tossing it back and forth, Peter and his friends saw a faint shadow growing larger and larger as it neared the boat, and were overwhelmed with fear. As the story goes, "And in the fourth watch of the night He came to them, walking on the sea. When the disciples saw Him walking on the sea, they were terrified, and said, 'It is a ghost!' And they cried out in fear. But immediately Jesus spoke to them, saying, 'Take courage, it is I; do not be afraid.'" (Matthew 14:25–27) Imagine being stuck in the middle of the ocean as the winds beat against your handmade boat, with a strange figure approaching you. The figure starts speaking, and it's speaking in your native tongue?! Nope. Nope. Nope! I don't care how far shore is, I'm making a run—well, I'm making a swim for it.

Unlike me, Peter spoke up. I would've been a little more skeptical with this being approaching me in the middle of a storm proclaiming Himself to be Jesus, but not Peter. Peter gave Him the benefit of the doubt. "Peter said to Him, 'Lord, if it is You, command me to come to You on the water.' And He said, 'Come!'" (Matthew 14:28–29). Peter stepped out of the boat and walked on the water below. There are many wonderings and interpretations of this story, namely about how Peter began to sink once he took his eyes off Jesus. The question I've never heard asked but will pose to you is this: Why did he go alone? No explanation is given as to why Peter went alone, but I have my thoughts. And the answer to that question is another key to unleashing the power within you, and unlocking your destiny.

To me there's only one valid reason. Others were too scared to go with him. I imagine Peter looking his friend Thomas in the eyes, but Thomas probably looked down to avoid making eye contact. Then he looked at James, and James probably faked like he was asleep the same way children do when they are too lazy to walk and want you to carry them upstairs. He looked at Matthew, and Matthew may have quickly replied, "Don't even bother asking." No one knows for sure, but I am fairly certain that the other eleven were too scared to join Peter and walk on water through the storm. Nevertheless, Peter still got out of the boat.

Sometimes, even when everyone else says no, you still have to go. Get out of the boat anyway. This will likely mean you have to go alone for the time being, and that's okay. **It's okay to go alone, so long as you go.** They say that fortune favors the bold, but that undersells the truth. History, destiny, and a new reality favor the bold as well. There are common phenomena that happen at theme parks or in large gatherings. Someone will be told a ride is scary, and will avoid it altogether even before trying it. In the midst of a large crowd, someone will see people seemingly running from something, and will begin to run as well. A similar phenomenon occurs in businesses: groupthink. Defined as "the practice of thinking or making decisions as a group in a way that discourages creativity or individual responsibility," groupthink kills creativity. It keeps you from doing what you think is best because you succumb to what others advise. You're hedging your bet; you're playing it safe; you're being logical. But playing it safe will never get you a gold medal. It won't give you a chance to walk upon the waves. If you play it safe you'll still be stuck on the boat, watching others change history.

When you're willing to get out of the boat and walk, history is made, and you can change your world along with the world around you. But you can't hesitate too long; you have to be willing to go, and you have to be willing to go alone.

Ruby attended class that whole year by herself. Her fellow white students refused to share a room with her and there was only one faculty member who was willing to teach a black student. But in the midst of loneliness and fear Ruby chose to wake up, get out of the boat, and walk. Day after day. Over time the school became more and more desegregated and years later Ruby's four nieces attended the same school. All because one woman, Ruby Bridges, was willing to get out of the boat.

Ruby Bridges now travels around the world sharing her story. I was in the sixth grade when I met her. She came to my school to speak, and she handed me a copy of her book and was kind enough to autograph it for me. Ruby Bridges changed my life that day and now I get to tell her story. Get out of the boat, change the world, change someone's life, and then watch as they tell your story too.

Be Illogical:

**Be the only one.** Peter was on the boat with eleven others, but he was the only one to walk on water. Sometimes your journey toward greatness will be lonely, but you **must** still take it.

**Get out of the boat.** Some will be scared of the peril that comes with chasing greatness. It may be a storm in the sea or a sea of individuals who disdain you for the color of your skin. Either way, if you want to change the world, you have to leave those who are scared behind and go anyway.

**Think long, think wrong.** There's a time to think through, ponder, and count the cost of every decision, but sometimes, you just have to go with your gut. Don't overthink it, be illogical.

It's okay to go alone,
## SO LONG AS YOU GO.

  #illogicalbook

# 13

## Scar Tissue

Scars remind us where we've been.
They don't have to dictate where
we're going.

—Agent Rossi on *Criminal Minds*

I suffered seven different bone breaks and muscle tears during the course of my combined eight-year collegiate and professional football career. Each one came with its own story and its own surgery. Each one was painful, but none was worse than at the NFL Combine, when I tore my quad thirty yards into my forty-yard dash.

I have done a lot of stupid things in my thirty-plus years on this earth. None more idiotic than trying to lose ten pounds in two days in order to run a faster forty-meter time. In cutting weight, from 238 pounds to 228 pounds, the morning of race day I was severely dehydrated. My thought process was simple—if I am lighter, I will run faster. But I forgot one universal truth: your body needs water to function. As a result, I tore my quad. The pain was immense. As I lay there ten yards away from the finish line, I cried, for the second time. I was so close; so close to reaching my goal. Now everything, including my draft stock, was in limbo. My idea of cutting weight didn't work. But in the end, I still got drafted, though as you recall far lower than I had hoped. But ultimately I was one of only 327 draft picks that year, and ended up being on the roster my first year in Cleveland. When you live a life based on being illogical, you'll have to make some illogical decisions. Sometimes, those decisions don't turn out how you thought they would. While I thought my dreams of being drafted were over after the gruesome injury, they weren't. I still got drafted. My dreams still came true.

My quad would eventually heal, but to this day when I rub my thumb over the quad muscle, I can still feel the scar tissue. It's an injury that I'll never forget. A vivid and palpable reminder that even though things didn't work out the way that I specifically planned, they still worked out.

The other injury that sticks in my mind most surprisingly happened off the field. In the fall of 2020 I had been doing more speeches, interviews, and podcasts than I could count. I was doing roughly two to three interviews a day, and on top of that a daily, two-hour TV show that I hosted. I had talked myself out of a voice. Literally, my voice was gone.

Not only did I lose my voice, I had popped a blood vessel in my vocal chords. I couldn't speak for days, doctor's orders. Not being able to talk is bad enough when you're the host of a daily show, but to top it all off, I was just four days away from what would prove to be the most important conversation to date. A conversation with one of the most powerful men in America. The man who runs the league that owns one day of the week each fall. A conversation with Roger Goodell.

Roger Goodell is the commissioner of the National Football League. He's the owners' boss and has the salary to match. The NFL had seriously mishandled several issues on race and I was scheduled to speak with the man who was ultimately responsible for all of those decisions. I had gotten on his calendar and booked my flight to New York to meet with him. Rescheduling was out of the picture.

This was the only time that Roger had on his calendar, plus, my schedule was only getting busier. The prognosis from the doctor wasn't great either. When I messaged her about my scheduling conflicts her response was disheartening. "Most times this takes three to four weeks to heal." I had three to four days. My only option was to take steroids for my throat, and not say a word until the day of the event. It could potentially cause more damage, but in my mind, it was worth it.

Four days, not a word. My colleagues thought that I had lost a bet. My family members thought I was ignoring them. My friends thought I was acting funny. But I wasn't. I was giving my wound some time to heal. There was no scar tissue yet.

The doctor prescribed a nebulizer, a breathing machine that helps soothe your voice. I used it every single day, every thirty minutes. The medicine coupled with the machine helped my throat recover enough to finally speak. Then, minutes before the conversation, I tested my voice. It was weak, but it worked. And thus, a conversation occurred.

I was so afraid. My moneymaker, my calling card, the only thing I needed to be successful at my job, had been taken away. And I had no idea if it was coming back. I didn't know what this popped blood vessel meant for my present, for my future. The pain was palpable, but the fear was frightening.

I rested my voice. I took off from work for a few days and reached out to a friend who had been through a similar experience. He recommended therapy: speech therapy. I needed to find a new way to talk without putting a strain on my vocal cords, so I met with this vocal coach two times a week as my throat began to heal. She taught me how to communicate by using my core: to boom with my belly. A lesson that I still use today. What once was an area of weakness has now become a strength for me. My voice is stronger than ever, but I needed a little bit of help.

When you're living an illogical life, you're going to run into your fair share of struggle. You'll be wounded in ways that words may not be able to express. You'll have weaknesses that wear you down.

Identify the wounds and the weaknesses and get the help you need. Take a break to recover when you need to, but keep moving forward toward your dreams.

I'll end with a harrowing story that, to me, is an incomparable example of the power of our scars, but I've also committed to tell it. She told me that "A-27,633" was her new name. She was no longer Tova Friedman. Her house was bombed on her first birthday. She wasn't home. Thousands were lined up and executed. She wasn't. Her group was the next in line to be gassed. They selected the wrong group. She arrived in town on Sunday, and the Germans wanted to wait until Monday for the next round of killings. Little food, no friends, and immense fear. There is no logical reason that she should still be alive today, but she is. Tova survived the Holocaust.

Tova Friedman is a sweet and petite Jewish woman, one of the youngest living Holocaust survivors, and I recently had the pleasure of spending a day in New York City with her and her family. She was born on September 7, 1938, in Gdynia, a port city in Poland.* On her birthday, her parents

_____

* https://www.preserveauschwitz.org/survivor/tova-friedman/

decided to take her to her grandparents' house about five hours away to celebrate. That's when the first bomb struck. The war had begun. Tova's home was destroyed. Her uncle was still back at the house. He didn't make it out.

Being a Jew in Europe during that time was dangerous. Adolf Hitler and the Nazi Party believed that Jews were subhuman. The Nazis believed that their race, the Aryan race, was superior. They wanted as much land, power, and dominion as possible. Getting rid of the Jews was the number-one goal. Tova was a Jew.

When the war began, she was housed with fifteen thousand other Jews in a ghetto. Six apartment-like buildings in a compound in Poland. Fifty people per one-bedroom apartment. There was no space, and very little food. For all intents and purposes, she lived under the kitchen table. There was no space anywhere else. Then, little by little, people started to disappear. She would go to sleep one night, wake up the next morning, and see fewer people than she saw the day before. They were being taken in the middle of the night. First it was the elderly. The Nazis were forcing the Jewish people to work, and the elderly were seen as least useful. One night, her grandmother and grandfather were there, the next they were gone. Tova recalls a day before she was taken in a cattle car to Auschwitz that the Germans invaded her home. She was enjoying porridge with her mother and father when a loud commotion arose outside. "Quickly hide!" her parents shouted. During this abduction, the Germans were looking specifically for children. As the Germans entered the room, their boots began to bang on the concrete floor, and Tova was afraid. Her mother squeezed her mouth so tightly to prevent her from making noise that she had blue and black marks around her jaw. Tova survived that day. But this was only the beginning.

At five years old Tova was forced to board a cattle car with her mother. Her father was stripped away from her family at that point as the men were forced to go a different direction. Women and children yelled as they were forced to board this train. They knew what this meant. Tova was headed to Auschwitz—"the final solution to the Jewish question."

While on the cattle car to Auschwitz, her mother prepared her. "Never look a German soldier in the eye. Never speak unless first spoken to and under no circumstance are you allowed to cry." Tova arrived and leaped off of the train; her small legs could not take the step. She stared straight ahead, her miniature frame meeting not only the waist of the German soldiers, but the dense drool and sharp teeth of the German shepherds. She was told to roll up her sleeve. "A-27,633, that is your new name," she heard from one of the Jewish women tasked with tattooing each child after they arrived. I asked Tova what happened to the woman who tattooed her; her response: "She was killed right after. She was given a job and after performing her duties the Germans had no more use for her."

Tova and her mother were separated. All the children were separated from the adults at that point, sent to different barracks. From her barrack she could see the gas chambers used for extermination. She told me, "I knew what went on there, but I didn't know anything else. Horror had been my whole life, I just felt like this was a rite of passage for Jews." The days went on as the Jewish children awaited their fate. Then one day it came; Tova and those in her barrack were told to head to the gas chamber. As they walked through the camp toward the chamber she heard her name. "Tova! Tova!" She was confused; she had forgotten her name because no one had used it in so long. She looked around searching for the familiar voice calling her and saw her mother. Her mother's arms reached through the bars that were holding all the women captive. "Where are you going, Tova? Where are you going?" Her mother questioned. "To the gas chambers!" Tova replied. Her mother trembled with fear from behind the bars.

Tova arrived at the gas chamber with the other children. She was set to die. "It was freezing cold and the German soldiers made us strip naked so we were all huddled together for warmth," Tova recalled. That's when she heard shouting in German as the soldiers began to argue with one another. "Go back to your barracks!" the guards yelled. The gas chambers were broken that day. As Tova walked back, her mother once again saw her and yelled, "Tova! What happened! What happened?!" Tova replied, "The chambers are broken, we're going back tomorrow!" There would be no tomorrow. At least not as a prisoner.

Shortly after the malfunction of the gas chamber, Russian soldiers arrived to overthrow the Germans. Tova would survive the greatest genocide in history.

As the Russians arrived the Germans made one final attempt to obliterate everything and anyone in sight. Jews scrambled toward freedom as German guards were no longer at their posts. Tova's mother sprinted around the camp in search of Tova, and when they were finally reunited they knew they had to hide until the chaos between the Russians and Germans subsided. The Germans paced the camp looking for any Jewish survivors to kill. That's when Tova made one of the most harrowing decisions I've ever heard. Tova hid with a corpse. As the Germans searched the barracks for any Jewish survivors to kill, Tova and her mother ran to the building acting as the mortuary. The stench was putrid. There were countless bodies inside on tables draped by blankets. Most were dead; others dying. Tova's mother searched for a corpse to place her next to, and after finding one Tova jumped onto the table and under the sheet. She hid facedown as to not breathe into the sheet and cause it to move. "As I held onto the body, I felt safe. The corpse wasn't dangerous. It was the one time someone wasn't trying to kill me," Tova recounted during our conversation. The decision to hide next to a corpse was crazy. The action, too frightening to even imagine. But the decision ultimately saved Tova's life.

When Tova and I met in New York we met at Wagner Park, overlooking New York Harbor and the Statue of Liberty. It reminds her of the freedom she was granted as she took a three-week-long boat ride from Germany to America. But Tova lives with an even greater reminder on a daily basis. One that she cannot escape, nor does she want to. A-27,633. The tattoo still remains on the wrist of her left arm. I asked her to see it during the course of our dialogue, and as she rolled up her sleeve my eyes met the numbers. In a naïve attempt to comfort her, I said, "Oh good, it's starting to fade." She quickly responded as though offended and said, "No, it's not, it's still as clear as ever. Look again. I can still see it. And even when I don't see it, I feel it." I was curious about her sharp response back to me; it was as though she was proud of her tattoo. So I asked her, "Why haven't you gotten it removed?" Her response changed my life, and it's one of the countless reasons I tell her story—I trust it will change yours as well. Tova said, "I like my tattoo. I'm proud of my tattoo. I wear all of my scars proudly. They remind me what I have been through. What I have survived."

When I sat down with Tova in May 2020 she asked that I always keep her story alive. I gladly accepted the responsibility to share the story of her scars. Tova's story is a story of unthinkable triumph, unimaginable pain, and unspeakable tragedy. But her parting message of her scars is one we should all cling to desperately. Our journeys will all look drastically different, hopefully none as gruesome as Tova's. But we will all have decisions to make, and the journey, regardless of its path, will leave us with scars. Embrace your scars; your scar is a reminder that you overcame. Your scar is a reminder of your survival. Your scar is a reminder of your triumph.

Be Illogical:

**It didn't work, but it will work out.** Things will not go as you planned. Allow me to say that again: things will NOT go as you planned. **But just because you have to take a detour doesn't mean you won't get there. Let the scar tissue serve as a reminder that you made it.**

**Patience is paramount.** If you've ever had to take a detour on the road while you're in a hurry, you know that your blood pressure will accelerate faster than your car. That is unless you consciously choose to exercise patience. Your journey to success may not be quick, so remember, patience is paramount.

**Influence with your scars.** We live a life based upon impressions. We desire to impress people and make our best first impression. But influencing someone is of greater value than impressing them. Be proud of your scars and use them to influence others.

Just because you have to take a detour doesn't mean you won't get there.
**LET THE SCAR TISSUE SERVE AS A REMINDER THAT YOU MADE IT.**

# 14

## How the Turtle Got There

When you see a turtle on a fence post, know that it did not get there on its own.

—ANONYMOUS

Born in 1867 and 1871 respectively, Wilbur and Orville Wright, also known as the Wright Brothers, are known as the first individuals to successfully fly a plane. They were Midwestern kids, hardworking and blue-collar. Gritty creators and investors. Both attended high school, but neither received a diploma. Instead they started their own printing business in 1889. Orville designed and built the printing press and his brother Wilbur assisted him. Together they launched a weekly newspaper where Orville would act as the publisher and Wilbur the editor. This printing press was the first of their endeavors, but it was far from the last.

By the late 1880s the two-pedal bicycle had started to gain widespread popularity. The brothers tapped into this newly robust industry and opened a bicycle repair and sales shop. By 1896 they began manufacturing their own bikes under their company, the Wright Cycle Company. Many would have been content with creating and sustaining two businesses, but for the Wright brothers this was just another crucial step on their way to conquering aviation.

By 1896, the Wright brothers' serious interest in flight and flight research took hold. They began meticulously studying birds, engines, and wings, trying to navigate the complexities of aviation. Just four years later they were testing their first plane. By 1903, they were flying. The first flight the Wright brothers took lasted just three seconds—the engine of the plane stalled out. But three days later they were flying over eight hundred feet in the air for nearly one minute. They had done it. The Wright brothers had done what most believed to be impossible at the time.

As a son of two Nigerian immigrants, I've always gravitated toward African proverbs. Now, while I don't know exactly what constitutes an African proverb, they ring true nonetheless. My favorite one reads as follows: "When you see a turtle on a fence post, know that it did not get there on its own." Now, I've never seen a turtle on a fence post, but after a quick Google search, you'd be surprised by how many images of turtles hanging out on fences appear. The meaning of the quote is quite literal. The turtles in these photos could not have climbed onto the fence post without the help of someone else. When Wilbur and Orville Wright were seen high above the ground, they didn't get there on their own either.

German aviator Otto Lilienthal is noted as the most influential glider pioneer. He began his research in 1871, making strides in the field until his tragic death while flying one of his planes in 1896. It was his death that motivated the Wright brothers to study aviation. They used many of Otto's methods and principles; his knowledge of wings and engines was strong, and he had made considerable progress in figuring out two of the three essentials for flight:

A set of lifting surfaces/wings.

A means of propulsion.

But he hadn't figured out the third: a method of balancing the aircraft. This meant the Wright brothers needed to fix their attention to balancing the aircraft. The brothers knew that Otto's method of balancing the aircraft with the pilot's body weight, shifting their weight to turn the aircraft, was limiting and dangerous. It's what led to Otto's death. They developed wings that were controlled by the pilot. The pilot could tilt the wings in order to change the direction of the craft. They had solved the final piece of the flight puzzle.

We hold the Wright brothers up as creative geniuses, which they undoubtedly were, but we must always keep a keen eye to the creative genius of those who existed before. Without Otto's research, we don't know when flight would have been achieved. Does this diminish the Wright brothers' achievements? Of course not. In fact, it was their ability to learn from and honor others that led to their success.

It won't be easy for you to soar in this life, and when you do, keep in mind you won't have done it alone. Keep your mind open to the creative genius of those who existed before you. Keep an attentive ear to the brilliance that exists around you. Learn from others' brilliance. Grow from others' genius. Use it to help you soar. The Wright brothers had childlike faith. Every child, and many adults, wish they could fly. The Wright brothers actually did. They had their "maybe I'm crazy" moment, I'm sure. It probably happened the second they strapped into the makeshift cockpit of their first flight. Unbeknownst to them they were tending to sheep as David did, but their sheep had no legs, only bicycle wheels. They experienced their first drop of rain during the course of the first flight, and obviously the dam broke. Every time you and I hop on a plane to go anywhere, we're a living testament to the breaking of the aviation dam.

Making it in the sports world is hard, but like a pacemaker in a long-distance race, I had someone to help lead the way. My older brother is a trailblazer. Highly competitive yet unreasonably relational, he taught me a lot. He was older, bigger, and stronger than me, so, as a kid, I always had to keep up. Since we were close in age, we always played on the same sports teams. It started with soccer. I was a four-year-old playing with a bunch of six- and seven-year-olds. Basketball and baseball followed suit. The same theme continued in the classroom. After attending a public school for grades one through four, I applied for a private school in fifth grade. My older brother served as a guide, never aiming to outshine me, but always aiming to set the bar high. He won Athlete of the Year at our high school, got full scholarships to multiple schools, started as a rookie in the NFL, and got his MBA while he was playing. Every time he succeeded, he left a less resistant path for me to follow. He set the bar for me to jump over, but also aided my ability to soar by taking the path before me.

When I could no longer follow my brother through football, I looked to someone else for help. Ande Wall is a former college basketball player turned ESPN producer. She and I met during my time in Austin. As soon as I had been released from the Eagles, I called her to ask for work advice. Maybe she could even offer me a job on TV. She saw my talent during a few brief interviews in college and wasn't afraid to give me a chance to develop it. Ande has a heart of gold. She's one of the kindest people I've ever met. She cares deeply for those around her and has a special place in her heart for former athletes. She knows how the system can chew you up and spit you out and she wasn't going to allow me to be another statistic. She gave me an audition, saw my potential, and hired me on the spot. I joined the Longhorn Network weekend show with a few other Texas athletes and developed my skills. But it didn't stop there. After I left Longhorn Network to go to ESPN, I would still send Ande my tape. She would watch it and give me feedback. Even now, with my daily show, she does the same thing. Ande gave me a chance. When I made the ask, she offered the help. Together we created something special.

Ande wouldn't be the only producer to help me get to where I'm at today. Pam Vaught is the news director for Fox 7 Austin. Since I was going to be in town and had some free time on my hands, I reached out to Pam and asked for an opportunity. I didn't know her and she didn't know me. I looked up her information online and sent her an email stating who I was and what my intentions were. Pam invited me in for an interview. I drove up to the studio, interviewed with her in an office downstairs, then left. I didn't know what to expect. I also didn't know how the industry worked. Then a few weeks later, I got an email back. Pam had reached out to her general manager and advocated for me to join the morning show. With her recommendation, "Mondays with Manny," a segment on *Good Day Austin*, began. I joined the Fox 7 Austin morning crew every Monday morning during the football season—a three-hour show. I always wanted to talk about more than just football. Yes, we talked sports, but we did so much more. We had fun, we made good TV, heck, I even got to cook on live television. For the record, I'm a much better cook when the cameras aren't rolling, I promise. I learned how to read from the teleprompters, address the camera, and interact with my colleagues on set. It was also there that I learned what goes into producing a show: blocks, content, commercial breaks, all of it. It was the opportunity of a lifetime, and Pam helped me get to where I'm at today. Pam helped me soar.

And then there's the help I received that made *Uncomfortable Conversations with a Black Man* what it is today. I was initially going to call it *Questions White People Have*. I could tell that there was a communication barrier between black people and white people and that barrier was costing black people their lives and white people their dignity. So, I called up a few of my white friends, along with Marcus Spears, a black colleague of mine from ESPN, and Rachel Lindsay, the first black lead on *The Bach-*

*elorette*. The plan was simple: meet up in Dallas, rent out a studio space, and answer difficult questions. Three black people and three white people, sitting around a table. The white people would ask questions and the black people would answer them. Marcus, Rachel, and my white friends agreed. The videographer agreed. COVID didn't.

Due to COVID-19 policies, Rachel wouldn't be able to fly to Dallas in time to record. Marcus was also finding it difficult to get time off of work. His employer required that he avoid contact with any groups of two or more. We were in a pandemic and I was in a time crunch. With protests in the streets and social media ablaze, this content was needed, now. So, I decided to scrap the initial plan and have a one-on-one conversation with one of my dear white friends who was still available. She drove three hours on a day's notice.

The day before the planned conversation, I took a walk. I do this often. To think, pray, and clear my mind. While I was walking, I got a text message. "Emmanuel," my friend began. "I'm on my way to Austin and have been thinking about our conversation for tomorrow. I've been talking to so many people from different backgrounds and they seem to have similar questions. My Indian friends, Asian American friends, and friends from different races all seem to have the same questions that some of my white friends have. Would you consider changing the title? Something like 'Uncomfortable Conversations' may be more inclusive." I didn't like it. "Uncomfortable Conversations" didn't have the ring to it that I was looking for. It wasn't sticky.

I walked back home pondering the title. I walked inside my house and past the full-size mirror in my living room. I took a few steps backward and looked at the mirror, staring into it. That's when it hit me. "I'm a black man, and the questions are uncomfortable. Uncomfortable Conversations . . . with a Black Man!" I texted my best friend Mo and shared the idea. She loved it. And thus, *Uncomfortable Conversations with a Black Man* was born with a new vision and much better name. I couldn't have been happier. And I couldn't have done it without help.

As for my friend who helped me change the name, she ended up not being able to join me at the last minute. I recorded it by myself. I was the only one in front of the camera, but I definitely wasn't alone. My best friend Mo was there the entire time. She was there for every recording, of every episode, in each city we recorded in. She helped me find the loopholes in my logic and the flaws in my reasoning. She also helped teach me the patience I needed to persevere along this journey. Especially when my temper ran short on those who didn't come through in the way that I expected. While you're being illogical, allow the people who believe in you to be there for you. Being illogical doesn't mean you have to be alone.

It never hurts to have a big brother, someone who can draft for you. I hope to figuratively be that for you. My brother taught me all he knew about not just playing, but succeeding at the next level. Once he was discovered, it made it easier for me to be discovered. Ande still coaches me today; I send her all of my clips and she gives me critical feedback. I take my earmuffs off for that. Pam is still doing her thing at Fox 7 as well. And as for my brother, who's recently retired from the NFL and is transitioning into a broadcasting career, let's just say I'm the one helping him right now. Life can be cyclical that way.

Anyone who accomplishes anything great in this life, whether it be conquering flight or following a personal dream, has followed the path of being illogical laid out in this book. I'm just defining the steps that must be taken. Don't miss this step. **Don't forget the help you will need along the way.** Ask for help, solicit help, heck, read self-help books. Ask the right questions of yourself and of others, then get on top of that fence post.

Be Illogical:

**Learn from your predecessors.** LeBron James is arguably one of the greatest basketball players in the history of the game and has long admitted that Michael Jordan, inarguably the greatest basketball player of all time (unless you're talking to a LeBron fan), was his idol growing up. LeBron learned from his predecessor, and when it's all said and done, he may surpass him as well. You and I should do the same for those that came before us.

**Ask for help.** A turtle can't speak, but if it could, you would have to imagine that after watching countless humans pass it by as it looked up at the fence post, it would finally claw at a pedestrian's shoe and make its plea for some assistance. I had to do the same thing. You're going to need some help along the way; don't be afraid to ask for it.

**Keep those who help you close.** Honor the people who aid you on your journey. Bring them with you. Reciprocate the help. You can't help each other if you aren't in it together.

**Say "thank you."** In March 2020, during the peak of the world's coronavirus pandemic, my agent masterfully negotiated a deal making me the newest cohost of a Fox Sports morning show. At just twenty-nine, I had finally journeyed to the top of the sports television mountain by becoming a mainstay on a national sports show. The moment I hung up with my agent, I proceeded to go through my phone alphabetically, texting all those who helped me along the way. The words I wrote to them are the same simple words I share with you for reading this book: thank you.

Don't forget the **HELP** you
will need along the way.

  #illogicalbook

# 15

## You Gotta Have "It"

He was already destined for the Hall of Fame. I was just a sixteen-year-old kid who was honored to be in his presence. He leaned forward in his chair and we locked eyes. His temperament was calm as could be while my heart was beating faster than I'd ever remembered. I was anxiously awaiting the words that would come out of his mouth. What he would say would dictate the next four years of my life and determine a majority of my future. With a southern Texas drawl he finally spoke, "Emmanuel, you have 'it' . . . you can't define it, but you know it when you see it. Welcome to the team." Those words changed my life. The man then proceeded to offer me a full scholarship to play football at the University of Texas. That man was Mack Brown, the head coach of the storied University of Texas football program. I was floored. Then, almost fifteen years later, Oprah said the same thing.

Oprah Winfrey is one of the most iconic women in the world. Beyond everything I told you about her nationally syndicated talk show in chapter 8, she was also the first black female billionaire. Media mogul, actress, producer, author, there's nothing that Oprah hasn't done. After sharing a brief Face-Time together about my intentions with the *Uncomfortable Conversations with a Black Man* series, Oprah asked me to join her for a conversation on her new show. I obliged. Because, duh! In the forty-five-minute virtual conversation, I fielded questions from ten individuals about race, justice, and what we as individuals could do to fight against racism. I had nothing written down and didn't know the questions beforehand. I was just in the zone. I responded in the only way I knew how: with empathy, honesty, and love. Oprah called me immediately after the screens turned off. I missed the call—I was still trying to recover mentally and emotionally—but thankfully her colleague Terry walked into my greenroom to congratulate me on a job well done. "Great job, Emmanuel, but, um, I think Oprah's trying to call you." I checked my phone and had a missed call from her private number. I rushed to call her back. She immediately picked up with excitement and before I could say a word she said, "Emmanuel! You've got the thing, my friend! You've got the thing! And coming from someone who had the thing and has the thing, you, my friend. You've got the thing!"

I was blown away. I responded to this media giant, in a somewhat confused tone, "Thank you so much, Ms. Winfrey, but, uh . . . what is . . . what is 'the thing'?" Her response echoed the sentiments expressed by my coach over a decade earlier.

"It's hard to describe it, but you know it when see it." I couldn't let her get away without telling me what "the thing" was. I still hadn't figured out what "it" meant, and now another Hall of Famer in her own field was again telling me I have some "thing."

I pressed her and asked again, "Can you describe the thing?"

She replied, "Hmmm, it's like you have this ability to tell people difficult and hard information, but they appreciate you for doing so. They want to learn more."

I'll never forget that moment, that call, those words. I literally have the quote saved in the Notes app of my phone. I review it from time to time whenever I begin to doubt myself.

This is all quite ironic because when I was in school, I spent a lot of time in detention. I would make quick-witted comments to peers and teachers and those comments would land me in the principal's office. It wasn't that I was trying to be disrespectful, I just didn't always agree with my professors and wanted to challenge the ways in which we thought or learned. I craved those tough and uncomfortable conversations that I felt would propel us to better learning and further understanding. Many of my professors saw this trait as disruptive and even arrogant. I still chuckle when I reminisce on my past. I thought football was my "it," but really talking was, even as a kid. How illogical that what I was punished for, many years later would be the "it" Oprah called to praise me about.

If all you've heard up to this point is that to succeed in life you must be illogical, then you've heard too much. While that statement is partially true, there's another necessary piece that is critical to your success. That piece is something known as "it." You gotta have "it."

This begs the question: What is your "it"? The answer to that question is simple. What is the thing that you're inherently good at or that you thoroughly enjoy? I'm not talking about the thing you kind of do well, but what is the thing you're naturally better than everyone else at or naturally inclined to do? For some it may be building. For others it may be being of service to those in need. For some, speaking or teaching. Others' "it" may be the ability to be patient with children or to take care of the elderly. The fact is, everyone has an "it." We just need to work on defining it. That's where I come in.

Defined by me, "it" is a predisposition to having an enhanced skill or being uniquely gifted at something. As a TV host, I've found that my "it" is the ability to communicate decisively and authoritatively when the camera comes on. I grew up the youngest son of a pastor, so I spent most of my time watching my dad communicate with large congregations of people. It took me decades to realize my "it," but I did have it. Noah had it too. His "it" was carpentry. Noah was obviously a skilled builder. If God were to ask me to build a boat, I'd drive straight to Home Depot and see if I could find work for hire. Otherwise, I'd tell God that he probably has the wrong person. I can hardly screw a light bulb in, let alone build a boat. David obviously had "it"—a keen sense of depth perception and pinpoint accuracy when using a slingshot. Even Roger Bannister had "it"—a higher number of slow-twitch muscle fibers allowing him to fatigue slower.

You don't have to be a superhero. You just need to take some time to find your "it," through testing things out and doing the things that you're naturally gifted at. Think for a second about your life. If you can answer the question of what you were naturally skilled at growing up or what you naturally gravitated toward, then you'll be closer to finding your "it." People always ask me, "Emmanuel, why'd you play football?" To which I reply, "Because I was six foot two and 240 pounds with enough speed and power to protect myself. If I were advanced at math, I would've been an accountant." You each have it; sometimes it may be tangible, sometimes it may not be. Sometimes it may be both. No matter how small or seemingly inconsequential your "it" might be, if you take the time, you will most certainly find it. And that's the first step.

But my "it," this ability to convey difficult information in a digestible way, didn't come out of thin air; it was passed down to me at an even younger age from a critical thinker, a great communicator, and a bold believer. My dad.

Dr. Onyebuchi S. Acho is a phenomenal orator. It was probably those idle buses in Nigeria he spent all that time preaching and teaching on. He knows how to communicate effectively and make things make sense. That was the gift that helped him come to America. He also knows how to be uncomfortable. It would be that gift that I would see at an extremely young age on the way to a village in Africa.

Nigeria was under military rule at the time. The president had died and there was a struggle for power. The military joined the struggle and decided to "take over" for a while. Armed guards filled the airports. Security guards swarmed the streets. It was scary. I was afraid. But my dad wasn't.

We had just landed and were driving from the airport to our house in the village when we got stopped at a security checkpoint. These checkpoints weren't really for security, but rather for extortion. These police officers would use their power to take money from civilians. The only option was to pay up. If you didn't, they would delay you, discipline you, or deter you from your destination. Delays could last hours. And if you didn't fork over a few dollars, threats of jail time would ensue. A threat was usually all it was, until one day, my dad had had enough.

I was sitting in the back seat of the '87 Peugeot when we were stopped. Protocol was to stick your hand out of the window and hand the officers some money in order to pass by smoothly. Think of it as a tollway, except there were no booths, and the attendants had AK-47s. My dad was frustrated. Upset that these military personnel who were supposed to protect the public had continued to corrupt the country. Costing people precious time and hard-earned cash. He stopped at the checkpoint, declined to give them the cash, and dared the officer to do something. The officer was appalled. He was shocked that someone would stand up to him. He wasn't used to it. He asked my dad for his "particulars": his license and registration. My dad said no. He had been checked three times in the last three miles and the previous checkpoint was within earshot. My dad knew it was a money grab and he wasn't about to allow it. The officer told him to get out of the car. That's when things got interesting.

What I remember most about that interaction was the yelling. I was five years old so my young mind didn't completely comprehend what was going on. I was in the back seat with my siblings while my mom sat in the front. "Just give him the money!" she pleaded. He wouldn't. The next moment would change the course of my life. My dad and this officer had moved toward the back of the car while the yelling continued. The next thing I knew, this military dude was pointing an AK-47 in my dad's face. My mom was screaming. My dad didn't blink.

I would learn later that he knew something that most people didn't. He had a great understanding of human nature and he knew that this man wasn't a killer, but a coward. Trying to steal from people who had less power than him. When the gun was pointed at his face, my dad called the officer's bluff. He stared him straight in the eye and dared him to shoot. He didn't. My dad got back in the car and we drove away. Not a word was spoken for the next six hours. Talk about uncomfortable. Talk about crazy.

Fear is an oppressor. Pointing a gun at you and telling you to give up all that you have. Your freedom, your finances, your future. Many of us succumb to our fears. It's logical. When you see someone with a gun to your face you do what they tell you to do. But my dad knew something about this situation that most didn't. He realized that cowards run when they get called out. Bullies bail. I grew up with that interaction plastered in my mind like a poster on the wall. The most uncomfortable conversation, the most courageous conversation I had ever witnessed.

That desire to stand up for the oppressed and speak out against injustice is in my DNA. It flows in my veins and was modeled to me at a young age. Conversations become a lot less uncomfortable with situations like that as the standard. But just as my dad taught me to be fearless, he also taught me to communicate well.

I once asked my dad what made him so different. I asked him why so many people from around the globe would come to his office and pay him to listen to their problems (he is a marriage counselor by trade). His response intrigued me. "Many counselors want to be your friend," he began. "They want to keep you as a client. That's not me. I'm going to tell it like it is. I have to. Otherwise people will keep on going down the wrong path while thinking that they're on the right one. I can't have that." I was amazed. He then proceeded to compare his style of counseling to spitting in someone's soup while they watched him do it. I wasn't so keen on the soup idea, but I got the picture. My dad knew how to deliver difficult yet vital information to the people who needed it most. He was the king of the uncomfortable conversation. It was in his blood. He also has a gift of communicating to large audiences. He pastors a church in Dallas and speaks at conferences all around the globe. I'll never forget us going back to Nigeria one year and watching him speak to a crowd of over six thousand. He was at ease. I was exposed, at a young age, to effective communication to large audiences. I saw it every Sunday at church and on some of these trips overseas. His teaching style, much like his personality, addressed the issues and never backed down from discomfort. He actually enjoyed the discomfort. He knew that getting through it would bring clarity to chaos, meaning to a miscommunication. I did too. He joked once that his audience in America would be much larger if he didn't have an accent. He found that while his style was successful, certain people couldn't handle his vernacular. Well, I've got the style and ditched the accent, and my audience has grown tremendously. I found my "it." I have "the thing." All thanks to my pops.

Once you find your "it," the thing you need to do next is develop it. The greatest shooter in the history of the game of basketball, Steph Curry, found his "it." Shooting the basketball is a talent he was predisposed to. His father, Dell Curry, retired from the NBA in 2002 as the all-time leader in points and three-point shots made for the Charlotte Hornets. It's no coincidence then that Steph Curry is the best three-point shooter in NBA history. It's in his blood. Just like being a public speaker is in mine. And since Steph Curry found his "it" early, he jumped at any chance to have a basketball in his hands; even more than one. Curry would often do a drill where he'd dribble two or even three basketballs at a time (talk about illogical). He wanted to be great. He wanted to master his craft. He would put up a ridiculous number of shots each day and stay on the court until he made each one. He worked daily to develop his "it" and that hard work paid off.

He's setting records, making history, and succeeding greatly.

The Wright brothers aren't too dissimilar. They had always been creative; they had always been builders. Their "it" wasn't their propensity for formal education, but rather the creativity that lay within them. Remember, they created their own printing press, and after that transitioned into building and repairing bicycles. Imagine if the Wright brothers never developed their "it." If they didn't spend that time creatively building and repairing bicycles, they may have never been able to fly. David's story is the same. He was predisposed to his "it" as a boy and continued to develop it in the dark. He and his sling became one and the same. He fought off animals who tried to hurt his flock, so a large human would turn out to be no problem. I did the same thing. From the conversations about sports to rooting out racism, I worked on developing my "it" constantly. The same goes for TV. You'd be surprised at the number of times I'll randomly call a teammate or friend and debate a sports topic with them. I make these calls because I want to develop my "it." All hard work leads to profit. Suffice it to say, if you neglect your "it," who knows the battles that could be lost or the opportunities that could be missed. You have to develop it.

So far, we've talked about finding "it" and developing "it." Both are essential, but they're not everything. If you want to take the limits off of your life, you need to invest in your "it," even before you think it will pay off.

Many see money or even time as finite resources. Only to be used for the things that matter. But investing in your "it" is worth the time, money, and resources, even if it seems costly.

I bought high-quality cameras and studio-grade lights far before any of my videos went viral. I made interesting content about dogs and Disney songs. I knew what I wanted to do and did whatever it took to get there. I studied topics, prepared thoroughly, and made sure to speak with precision; and *this* skill I learned from one of my favorite artists.

Jamie Foxx is an actor, musician, producer, and executive. He loves to play the piano. He tells a story of getting a chance to play with the late Ray Charles. Once, while playing a duet with his idol, Jamie's fingers touched the wrong key. "Now why'd you go and do that?" Ray asked. Nervous, Jamie responded,

"I don't know, man, I guess I just messed up." Ray wasn't having it. "It's not about messing up," he said. "Take the time to play the right note . . . all the keys are underneath your fingers." I watched that interview and left forever changed. I realized that playing the right note, or saying the right words, cannot be rushed. You may only have one chance; when you get it, maximize it. Take the time to play the right note. That time, for some, may be finding the right words to respond in an argument. For others it may be reading the history of that industry you want to revitalize. For Steph Curry, it was setting aside time to dribble his basketball; buying rehab equipment to take care of his body. For the next Denzel Washington, it may be rehearsing that line over and over again until it's etched in your brain. Whatever your "it" is, you've got to invest in it. Put the time, money, and mental capacity toward it. It will be worth it.

These three attributes are important, but only penultimate. You can find "it," you can develop "it," you can even invest in "it." But this entire book, your entire life would fall short if you did all of that, but never did the last thing, the most important thing. You have to make a conscious decision; a decision that will change your life forever. You have to *use* "it."

Deciding to use your "it" is one of the most important decisions you will ever make. The life you've always wanted to live will depend on it. Your future generations depend on it. Millions have found their "it," hundreds of thousands have developed their "it." Thousands have even invested in their "it." But it's the few world changers who use their "it."

**The key to changing your life is to use your skills, your talents, your gifts. We are all gifted in something**, but we don't all use our gifts. Christmas is my favorite holiday, not only because of the meaning, but because I love gifting those I cherish. But think about it: What is the point of fighting the long Christmas lines, buying a gift, wrapping the gift, but never actually gifting it? That's what you're doing when you don't use your "it." You're like the wrapped Christmas gift that has yet to be opened. You're wasting something of precious value.

Many people are afraid to use their "it" because they know how much it will cost. And when I say cost, I don't only mean money. I mean friendships, family members, and in some ways, freedom. Let's go back to the story of my dad. He found his "it" as a teenager: telling people about the realness of God in a bold yet digestible way. It was a gift, but many laughed at him for it. He didn't know if it would

take him anywhere, so he had to make that courageous decision that we all will have to make at one
point or another. He was either going to follow his
"it" or follow someone else's logic.

He made the right decision and over half a cen-
tury later, generations and groups of people are ben-
efiting from it. Oprah, the Wright brothers, Steph
Curry, and Steve Jobs can all relate. You can too. We
all have a decision to make. And that decision point
can come with consequences.

Consequences exist for action but they also exist
for inaction. As a matter of fact, a "consequence"
is simply a result or effect of an action or decision.
They can be either positive or negative. And the
consequence for not using your "it" could be costly.
Noah's family and all the animals would've died;
Goliath would've won; nobody would have cool
phones; you get the picture. Don't be afraid. You
found it, you developed it, you've even invested in
it, now use it.

If I didn't ever use my "it," if I didn't ever speak
up against injustice, who knows what opportunities
I would have missed? I never would have hosted
*The Bachelor*; I never would have written a book. I
probably wouldn't be writing this one either. Find
your "it." Find your scientific anomaly. Find your

uniqueness. And double down on it. You don't need to walk away from the table; all the cards you need are right in the palms of your hands.

Be Illogical:

**Find "it."** We were all born with natural gifts, things that just come easy to us. For sprinters, like Usain Bolt, they were born with a higher count of fast-twitch muscle fibers. The accountant was predisposed to skills in math. The speaker was predisposed with oratory skills, or what I call "the gift of gab." You too have tangible or intangible skills that, when harnessed, excel beyond your peers. So, find your "it."

**Develop "it."** When David picked up his five stones as he prepared to slay Goliath he was without fear for a few reasons, the primary being he knew he was a bad man with that slingshot. He had developed his "it" so when the moment came, he was ready. Make sure you also develop your "it."

**Invest in "it."** Use the time, focus, money, or resources to invest in your "it." Go all in on your "it." It may seem illogical, too costly even, but your investment will pay off in more ways than you can imagine.

**Use "it."** "Faith without works is dead." You can find your "it" and develop your "it"; you can even invest in "it," but if you never act on "it," you've wasted your life.

The key to changing your life is to use your skills, your talents, your gifts. **WE ARE ALL GIFTED IN SOMETHING.**

#illogicalbook

# Epilogue

## The Theory of Everything

Hate, it has caused a lot of problems
in the world, but has not solved one
yet.

—MAYA ANGELOU

This book is risky; it's based on the theory that logic limits. But the fact is, everything in life is a theory, until it's proven. Everything in life is impossible, until it's not.

I wrote this book before the pandemic, before having my own show on TV, before the Emmy wins, and far before having a single uncomfortable conversation, let alone a number-one bestselling book. I had aspirations, then filled in the blanks as the impossible that I chose to believe unfolded. Everything in this book I believe in the depths of my soul. Why? Because I've lived it. Each chapter, each example, each illogical idea was dreamed far before it ever happened. Did I know exactly how it would turn out? No—but I stepped up to the battle line. I focus on starting, not finishing. That's the great thing about creating art in everything you do. You begin with a dream in mind and let the paint do the work. You let the dream continue to manifest. No goals, no limits, no logic. Cast it to the wind.

People may read these pages and think that being illogical is a decision set aside for the few, the unique, the special. Some may think, "This is easy for you to say, Emmanuel. You have a platform and I don't. You have certain abilities and I don't." Don't believe the lie. Don't buy the hype. Don't take the easy route. It's too logical. You have "it." It's time to embrace it. It's time to live out the thing you've been dreaming about for years. It's time to wake up.

Break the dam. The reason I wrote this book, the reason I broke my own four-minute mile, was so you could too. I chose an illogical lifestyle to show you that it can be done. That it's real. I wrote this book to bridge the gap between "im" and "possible"; between "ir" and "rational"; between "im" and "perfect." I stepped up to the battle line to get rid of the prefixes.

**If you remove the prefixes from "impossible," "irrational," and "imperfect," you're left with three powerful words: Possible. Rational. Perfect**. You see, prefixes change the meaning of the word but they don't get rid of the original word. The initial words, the words before the change, are still there and they are filled with power: possible, rational, perfect. They always have been. But somewhere down the line, when we stopped having childlike faith, we placed these prefixes on our words and also our lives. Since then, everything changed.

By now you've read the word "illogical" 126 times in this book. You've likely read it as one seamless word every time. I never do. When I see the word "illogical," I see "ill" along with "logical." Because I am ill of logic. I am sick of it.

Though in many spaces I'm the youngest, I still

lead. I was the first to play football in my family, then my brother followed suit. We both made it to the NFL. I was the first to get into media, now we're both on TV. Not just for family, for friends too. I want us all to win.

I've had more failures than successes in my life. Before the Emmy wins and bestselling books, there were major letdowns and puddles of tears. I was sad, lonely, frustrated, and afraid. But somehow, someway, after a major negative, something better followed. But to see that I had to refuse to let logic define the situation.

There are chapters that still need to be written, walls that still need to fall, logic that still needs to be defied. Those are things for you to do. By no means am I an expert, but I'm learning. I'm learning to be more and more illogical every single day. I hope you are able to learn with me and carry this work forward in your own lives.

Finally, I need to send a special message to you, reader. I want to thank you. Thank you for picking up this book, thank you for joining my conversations, thank you for watching my show, thank you for believing. Everything I do, I do for you. The content, the conversations, the commitment to excellence is solely for your benefit. I'm not a bestseller, we're bestsellers. I'm not having uncomfortable conversations, we are. It takes a village. Everything I do is with you in mind. With that being said, I would like to share with you one last dream. I had it seven years ago.

During my last year playing in the NFL, I was lying down in a hotel room. It was the night before the last game of my final season playing professional sports. All of a sudden, words came into my mind. I couldn't sleep, nor could I shake the phrase. I just kept hearing the phrase over and over. It seemed special, really special. So I grabbed my phone, opened up the Notes app, and began to type. I knew what I was writing was impactful, so I wanted to save it for the largest audience, the most important people I would ever come in contact with. I wanted to save it for you.

OPUS GLORIA

*My desire is to inspire / those to go higher / past the required / so those they admire / can also admire / whom they've inspired / before they expire*

The purpose of illogical thinking and living has always been to inspire you to go beyond what's required of you, so that I can admire what you do before I die. It's your turn now. Imagine a life without limits.

If you remove the prefixes from "impossible," "irrational," and "imperfect," you're left with three powerful words: **POSSIBLE. RATIONAL. PERFECT.**

# Acknowledgments

I'm not gonna lie: the acknowledgement section is my favorite part of the book. There's no pressure, no word count, and you can just say what you want to who you want. So where do I want to start. . . .

Let me start by thanking you, the reader. I've learned during my own journey that being illogical sounds great as a book title, but it is much harder to put in practice. However, if you've made it this far into the book, you've fully committed to being illogical and becoming the best version of yourself. For this I thank you, because I now get to watch you change the world.

To Oprah, once again I can honestly say I never thought I would be thanking you in my life, particularly because I never thought we would speak or that you would know who I am. However, I have quickly realized that good people are attracted to good things. I played team sports my whole life, and I can still confidently say you're one of the best teammates I've ever had.

To my brother Sam, the days sharing the football field with you were some of the most special moments I've ever had, but they went by far too quickly. It was a blessing to be able to partner with you again on this book.

Bryn, thanks for picking up this project in the middle of the madness and helping see my vision through. I look forward to working with you again. . . . Uh oh, that means I'm writing another book. We'll see!

Meredith, I told you I was going to tell on you in this book (see acknowledgement section of *Uncomfortable Conversations with a Black Man*). You are the best, here are ten thank-yous since I've surely forgotten to say it a time or two over the last year. Thank you, thank you, thank you, thank you, thank you, thank you, thank you, thank you, thank you, THANK YOU.

Terry, you saw in me what I hadn't yet seen in myself: the passion and ability to take a positive message to the world. Thanks for believing in me.

Mo, I'll once again say maybe this book could have been written without you, but I don't want to imagine how. Thank you for everything.

Steph, your love for me doesn't go unnoticed. You've always wanted to see me win, and you were the first one to speak my current reality of life into existence. Thanks for believing in me before there was much to believe in.

Chichi, you're forever one of my favorite humans on the earth. When my life got chaotic, our conversations about nothing and everything all at the same time kept me sane. I can't imagine my life with you. You're the best.

Dad, you taught me how to dream big. You taught me how to be illogical. You taught me that it's only crazy until you do it. Thank you for doing it, thank you for showing me the way.

Mom, you're an angel walking the earth. Thanks for being my biggest cheerleader and biggest supporter. Thanks for always making sure that your youngest son felt loved and taken care of. I love you.

Lastly, I end this book with the way I start anything I do of significance: by thanking God. I've consistently referred to this season in my life as my "Esther moment" (Esther 4:14). I'm honored that God equipped and called me to be a messenger in this moment. Jesus' love for me has set the bar for the way in which I'm called to love people, and the way in which I'm called to love you, the reader.

## About the Author

**Emmanuel Acho** picked up a football and made it to the NFL. He picked up a pen and became a *New York Times* bestselling author for *Uncomfortable Conversations with a Black Man*, followed by the #1 bestseller *Uncomfortable Conversations with a Black Boy*. He picked up a microphone and won a Primetime Emmy for his groundbreaking online series, *Uncomfortable Conversations with a Black Man*, amassing more than 90 million views to date. All this by the age of thirty, because of his ability to think and act illogically.

Emmanuel, the son of Nigerian immigrant parents, grew up in Dallas with his three siblings. He is a 2021 Sports Emmy winner, Fox Sports analyst (cohost of FS1's *Speak for Yourself*), and television personality. He is a former NFL linebacker and has a master's degree in sports psychology from the University of Texas.